WETLAND
ECOSYSTEM
T E A M

UNIVERSITY OF WASHINGTON

FEROX TROUT
AND ARCTIC CHARR

The world record rod-caught trout – a ferox of 17kg (37lb 6oz) 105cm (3ft 5in) taken by Mr Kurt Stenlund of Malmberget, Sweden. It was caught on a plug. (*Olle Öhman*)

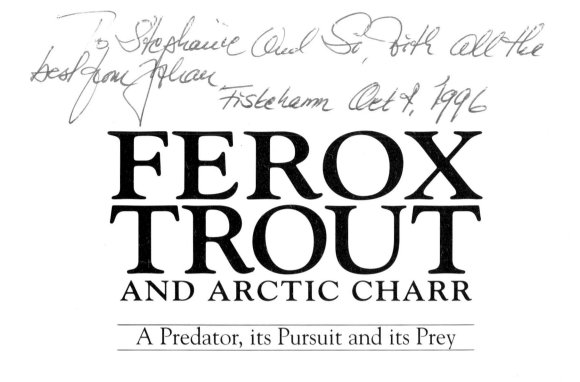

To Stephanie and Si, with all the
best from Julian
Fiskehamm Oct 9, 1996

FEROX TROUT
AND ARCTIC CHARR

A Predator, its Pursuit and its Prey

RON GREER

With the best wishes
of the author
Ron Greer Jun. 1996

SWAN·HILL
PRESS

First published in the UK in 1995
by Swan Hill Press an imprint of Airlife Publishing Ltd

British Library Cataloguing in Publication Data
   A catalogue record for this book
   is available from the British Library

ISBN 1 85310 486 8

Typeset by Hewer Text Composition Services, Edinburgh
Printed in Great Britain by Butler & Tanner Ltd, Frome and London

Swan Hill Press

an imprint of Airlife Publishing Ltd
101 Longden Road, Shrewsbury SY3 9EB

Contents

Foreword

Ron Greer is a man whose heretical views suit neither modern convention nor modern authority, not that fear of either could moderate his powerful eccentricity. From boyhood, when his grandfather taught him to catch sticklebacks in the back streets of Glasgow, his interest took him to work at the Freshwater Fisheries Laboratory at Faskally where he acquired his knowledge of Arctic Charr and his dedication to cannibal trout. In 1985 he founded the Ferox-85 Group.

In his youth he was to be found in his spare time hitch-hiking up the roads of Scotland with bags of trees on his back, planting them at random on countless verges. For his work with the Loch Garry Tree Group he won *The Times* Conservation Award.

It is this combination of deep love for the Scottish land and his conviction that its health is tied to native woodland and clean water that makes his book an essential read for anyone interested in the countryside. It may ruffle the feathers of conventional anglers, but the philosophy which it embraces deserves a wider public than those who sit with frozen fingers in boats on storm-tossed lochs, hoping to catch the biggest fish that ever lived.

PATRICK GORDON DUFF PENNINGTON

Dedication

I first met Bruce Macauslan in December 1984 in a hotel in Fort William, after I had presented a seminar on aspects of the biology of Ferox and charr as part of an extra-mural program run by the University of Aberdeen. It was a meeting that quite literally changed my life, and that of quite a few others too. Bruce had a knowledge and love of angling that was archetypal in nature. He combined these qualities with an ebullient capacity to share with others not only his hard-won experience, but also his sheer enthusiasm for the sport. This was especially apparent in his concern for children and young people starting out in the sport; many youngsters in Fort William owe much to him for starting them off on the right path. He also applied his considerable energies to the early development of the Ferox-85 Group and its sojourn after the record trout. Bruce was a huge man both metaphorically and literally. His contribution to the Ferox-85 Group was likewise. Sadly he never lived to see the end of the angling odyssey that had its rudimentary beginnings over a dram that winter evening. We often still feel his presence on our trips, and always the benefit of his knowledge and instruction. This book is gladly dedicated to his memory and passion for angling for Ferox. Thanks a million, Bruce.

Acknowledgements

No work of individual creation is wholly due to one person. Even Leonardo da Vinci had to use materials hewed and manufactured by unknown artisans and labourers. Pelé, even at his best, was dependant on ten other players to create the conditions for the expression of his skills. Writing a book is no less a team performance than a game of soccer, but there is no way that I am the literary equivalent of that great Brazilian soccer maestro! Therefore I have had to depend on the skills and abilities of many other people to produce this, my first book.

The greatest debt I have in acquiring the basic knowledge to contemplate this task is owed to those kind and erudite Scandinavians who made my trips to their beautiful boreal paradise so enjoyable and instructive. In this respect I have particular thanks to give to Professor Per Aass and his family, who initiated me into the Norwegian Ferox and charr experience. This debt of gratitude is equalled by that which I owe to two Swedish members of the International Society of Arctic Charr Fanatics, namely its founder, Dr Johan Hammar (not forgetting his wife Eva), and Professor Lennart Nyman, a Celtophile Welsh speaker with a great love of Scotland. Johan – as well as providing much basic data, detailed insights from his own vast experience, and photographs from his huge photo library – became a mentor and social worker during a long dark winter when I needed moral support during my many bouts of self-doubt in the course of writing the book. Telephonic support was also provided by fellow charr fanatics Drs Fred Kircheis and Ellysar Baroudy. Canadian charr fanatics Professors Geoffrey Power and Mark Curtis also chipped in here and, as did Fred, made my visit across the Atlantic as revolutionary to my thought processes as my trips to Scandinavia. I of course owe much to all the other members of ISACF for giving me a perspective on charr in their countries, especially Sasha Chernitksky, our 'mother hen' in Russia.

This group and individual support is only rivalled by my long-suffering friends in the Ferox-85 Group who eventually forgave me for trying out my literary thoughts on them. I am especially indebted to Aya Thorne for his scale reading work and of course the 'provision' of the British record trout. Moral support was also freely given by the Fairline Video team and, of course, by the direct contribution of Paul Young who was the first to support my outline proposal and to suggest how to take the idea forward. Technical support in the field was kindly given by Normark Sport Ltd, Daiwa Ltd and Partridge of Redditch. Without their help many samples of Ferox would not have been available. The Springbank Whisky Distillery's psychological support in kind is greatly appreciated for making even the worst of the blank days enjoyable, and the end of a spell on the word processor something to be looked forward to! Many thanks to the Loch Rannoch Conservation Association for their help in stationing boats on the loch.

The physical production of the drafts of the book were only made possible by my business partner and very long-suffering friend Derek Pretswell, who saw me through my failures in computer competency and is the only person to know just how hard it was for me to complete the work during a very difficult series of personal circumstances. The only other person to have an inkling of this is Colin McKelvie, the consultant editor, who saw a complete tyro through to completion of the task. Without his patience and advice nothing would have happened. Finally I owe a great deal of thanks to my father, George Greer, for starting me off in angling all those years ago. I must also not forget the contribution of that ex-boss of mine, whose sheer and utter negativity to Ferox and charr research made me all the more determined to succeed.

Introduction

In the spring of 1973 I began a study of the ecology of Arctic charr in Loch Garry and Loch Ericht, which lie in the Central Highlands of Scotland near the county borders of Perthshire and Inverness-shire. After setting my newly imported Scandinavian gill-nets I repaired to a 'wayside hostelry' in the town of Dalwhinnie to await their retrieval next morning. During my stay I fell in with a group of local worthies who, on finding out the purpose of my visit, regaled me with stories of fishing in the lochs. Their whisky-lubricated accounts were dominated by the capture and loss of giant trout – Ferox. Imbibition of our national drink notwithstanding, there was no real reason to doubt their truthfulness for their conversation revealed a detailed knowledge of angling techniques and there was also photographic evidence in support. I was however, as a professional biologist, strained to the limits of credulity on hearing their explanation for the occurrence of the 'Ferox phenomenon', namely that the fish was a hybrid between a pike and a salmon! Being a very open-minded sort of guy and in the process of drinking a good malt whisky at the time, I stifled my immediate reaction, both to save spilling the whisky and having my nose punched. The former would have been the more disastrous to mankind.

I felt however that my profession, with a few notable exceptions such as Dr Niall Campbell, had failed the majority of anglers. Somehow or other the biological reality of Ferox had not been revealed sufficiently well to the ordinary angler. There was myth, legend and pure simple bigotry in abundance, but where was the truth? I then remembered the famous quotation from the John Wayne/Jimmy Stewart Western *The Man Who Shot Liberty Valance*, where the reporter from the newspaper on hearing the truth of what happened said: '*When the myth becomes legend, print the legend.*'

Ever since I was introduced to trout angling by my father and his friends as a boy in 1950s Glasgow, I had been hearing myths and legends of the huge trout of the Highland lochs. Occasionally while visiting the tackle shops of the town centre with my father, we would see the odd photograph of a Ferox, or better still for me a glass-case specimen. Compared to the willing small perch from the Forth and Clyde canal at Dullatur or the rare capture of an 'ordinary' trout from the Clyde itself at Carstairs, these were for me monsters of fantastic proportions. It was the beginning of a fascination with Ferox for me, only partly satisfied by playing with my pre-Spielberg dinosaurs and graduating to pike fishing as I grew older. I became an avid reader of fishing books that had anything in them about Ferox, always dreaming of the day when I would finally get a chance to fish for them.

The books were full of angling lore and a scattering of black and white photographs of long-ago leviathans. Comments on the natural history and biology of the Ferox were rather limited and mainly dealt with their fish-eating propensity, and the large sizes obtained. More rarely some comments on the relationship of Ferox to other forms of trout and the classification systems of various authors appeared. This limited access to the literature also revealed the interesting dichotomy of attitude anglers and journalists had to Ferox. Love-hate relationship would partly fill the bill, but it also seemed much more than that. Ferox seemed to 'inhabit' that part of the human psyche where also lurked the wolf, shark and bear. On one hand there was a fascination with their predatory behaviour and large size, whilst on the other there was a type of revulsion that often lead to phrases such as 'ugly ,toothy, big brute of a fish' in descriptions. The photographs and mounted fish often countermanded this, but prejudice dies hard in the heart of any bigot, especially in angling!

I found the popular angling literature to be full of myths and legends about Ferox and few real facts about their biology. I felt let down somehow. No wonder that the explanation I was given as to the origins of Ferox that night in Dalwhinnie could come easily to the imagination of anglers. The myths and legends are fine and great fun, but there just *had* to be more.

Luckily for me I was eventually able to combine the professional and pleasure interests of life in one of those twists of fate that lead you to believe that the path you go down in life is pre-determined. In March 1969, after a rather unhappy spell as a laboratory technician in a Glasgow hospital, I took up a position as a scientific assistant at the Freshwater Fisheries Laboratory, Pitlochry, in Perthshire. Over the next twenty-three years I was in the happy position to be in one of the most richly endowed areas of the country for Ferox fishing. At the same time I was able to satisfy my thirst for knowledge on Ferox through some direct research, the studies of colleagues and access to an excellent scientific library. Quenching that thirst has of course proved impossible, but always fascinating and enjoyable remains the attempt. This is only rivalled by involvement in research on Arctic charr, the main prey of Highland Ferox and my personal route to a better understanding of them. Without that fanaticism and passion for charr this book would never have been written.

This book is, however, not just about fish. It is about people, those with a passion for Ferox, and I have been fortunate indeed to have worked and fished with two record holders. Dr Niall Campbell, whose scientific and popular writings inspired and educated me; and Alistair Thorne (Aya), whose technical skills surpass my own. There are many others too whom I will probably never meet who share this 'Ferox fever'. These people, the fish they pursue and the environment that supports their activities, deserve a better press than they have had hitherto. The myths and the legends will persist and grow, and so also must knowledge. Hopefully this book will enhance all three. In trying to do so I voice only my own personal viewpoints and though I have drawn heavily on the experience of others, the views expressed do not represent any organisation or group I am involved with. If you are upset by these views then I think perhaps you deserve the disturbance. Perhaps if nothing else they will give an answer to those bigots who still write off one of our premier sporting assets. There is of course still a lobby of opinion on Ferox whose attitude could be summed up as 'never mind the reality, I have closed my mind'. The dedicated Ferox angler will meet many of this type, but he or she can console him or herself with the knowledge that these poor lost souls will never know the thrill of that first encounter with the last of our 'Ice Age megafauna'.

-PAUL YOUNG

Don Greer

Preface

This is a book written by a man who is fired with that magical mix of a passion for the hunt of one particular species of fish, the Ferox, heightened by a scientific knowledge of its habitat and background. So passionate is he, that with a few like-minded friends, he formed the Ferox-85 Group, dedicated to the capture of this fine fish, with the ultimate goal of capturing a new British record brown trout.

Ron's experience, both as an angler and scientist give him a unique perspective to write about a fish that in many ways mirrors the human condition in Scotland in the present day; what we have done to ourselves and our country, we have also inflicted on the Ferox. His scientific research is fascinating and tells of ill-advised human 'improvement' that may have changed our flora and fauna for the worse, but his love of the fish itself and his ideas for improvement of the Scottish countryside and the waters that hold Ferox give optimism for the future.

Fishing for Ferox is not a passion to be undertaken lightly, and weather, tackle, logistics and profitable areas are all explored in Ron's amusing, succinct and cogent way. He is passionate and relentless. And therein lies the secret. He cares and is willing to put in the hours. Because hours means prizes and in April 1993, he witnessed the Ferox-85 Group capture that ultimate prize – the new British record brown trout, taken from Loch Awe. He suggests that fishing for Ferox can be a bum-numbing and brain-numbing experience. The former I'll give you, but I would suggest, that under Ron's stewardship, each member of the Ferox-85 Group is encouraged to keep their brain firmly in gear.

I first heard of Ron Greer as the man who was planting trees beside a Scottish loch to encourage a return to the old days when Scotland was covered with decidious woodland, not the newly introduced non-indigenous pines. The scheme had already brought frogs back to the waterside. I liked what the man stood for immediately.

We first met when filming *Hooked on Scotland* and I liked him even more. He spoke wisely of the whole Scottish angling condition, not just of his beloved Ferox. And knowing Ron and his fellow members, I am in no doubt that the Ferox-85 Group will soon beat the twenty pound barrier and thirty is by no means beyond their abilities.

Ron sometimes wears silly hats out on the water, but under them is a wise angling and scientific brain. Though he drinks a lot of coffee, he also has a liking for Scottish malt whisky. That will do for me.

You'll enjoy this book.

PAUL YOUNG

1

Ferox, the Aquatic 'Wolf' from the Ice Age

The analogy of the Ferox and the wolf – and their respective prey, charr and reindeer – is possible and apt because both sets of predator/prey relationships, and indeed the present physical forms of the animals themselves, owe their derivation to the series of cataclysmic climatic events we know of as the successive Ice Ages of the Pleistocene Era. We humans also owe much of our own cultural and physical evolution to the challenge presented by this phenomenon. Today we are largely insulated from its effects by the cocoon of our modern urban and industrial society. In the British Isles, only those people living in the rural areas of Scotland, Ireland, England and Wales north of the 'Tees-Exe line' experience the physical limitations and opportunities presented by the successive advances and retreats of the glaciers. The whole structural backdrop of the country in which the races and cultures of northern Britain have functioned over the millennia is a product of the climatic processes of the Pleistocene. If we tend to neglect or forget the importance of the Ice Ages in our own evolution, we cannot deny it relative to our past and present flora and fauna, or indeed to that of other areas of the northern hemisphere similarly affected by glaciation.

Enthusiasts and specialists have long appreciated the rich and interesting floristic inheritance of the Arctic–Alpine plant communities of the British and Irish mountains where, to a large extent, the Ice Age has never completely gone away. These so-called relict species are of major conservational value and often are the subject of a plethora of protective official designations. Bird lovers have likewise done much to promote public appreciation of the value of northern bird species such as bunting, dotterel and ptarmigan, species again indicating the affinities between British uplands and Arctic regions. Any well-informed student of British mammalian species could also easily point out past and present connections to the northern fauna of Eurasia and North America. Only our own greedy short-sighted folly, manifested in habitat destruction and over-hunting, robbed us of the northern faunal inheritance of moose, brown bear, reindeer, beaver, wolf and lynx etc. (There is even some evidence to suggest that if it were not for our own actions the mammoth would have remained with us too!) The British have treated this rich inheritance carelessly, and our track record suggests that the remaining elements are not yet safe.

Pretty plants, beautiful birds and amazing mammals capture our imagination and sympathy fairly readily for a number of reasons, not the least of which is their tangibility. Without too much trouble we can touch them, walk up to them, photograph and even, within certain legal constraints, collect them because they share the terrestrial world with us. Fish, on the other hand, live in a different medium to us, an alien aquatic world largely distant and unknown to most of us. People generally find it easy to identify with the problems of conserving our land-based wildlife, especially if it has beautiful blossoms or 'Bambi-like' babies. Fish, unfortunately for them and fish enthusiasts like myself, do not appeal anything like as much. We should however realise that the Ferox and charr populations of the British Isles are an integral part of our inheritance of the great northern fauna of Europe and Fennoscandia. Whilst the Great Irish elk fought for survival against a pack of wolves in the drainage basin of the Shannon, or huge bull reindeer battled for herd supremacy on the shores of what is now Loch Shin, Ferox and charr were enacting their own part in the Ice Age drama. Unlike the other 'players' this act is still on stage and we are indeed fortunate to have it so. In Ferox, and to an even greater extent in charr, we have a relatively intact resource and one about which very little is known. There is in my experience no such thing as an expert on Ferox. If you meet someone who purports to be one then the person is either suffering from a surfeit of drink or is suffering from delusions of competence.

The special position of Ferox and charr in our Arctic fauna reflects the general propensity in the family Salmonidae for survival and wide distribution in the northern hemisphere. It is a family of fishes that has long interested fish scientists in a number of different disciplines. This interest is in large part derived from the adaptive capacity of the various members of the family in some of the harshest environments of the north. In adapting to the consequences of continental drift and especially to the repeated evolutionary challenges presented by glaciation and deglaciation, this group of fishes has developed a large number of sub families, genera, sub-genera, species, sub-species and races that have intrigued fish taxonomists (those who classify fish) for centuries. To the uninitiated this can appear very bewildering and, frankly, no study will help you to catch any more fish. Yet it is satisfying to have some schematic overview to understand better the overall relationship Ferox have with their near relatives.

Scientists vary in their summaries and to the present day are still arguing intensely about the relative position of various components of the family tree. Generally there is fairly good agreement about the positions of the more distantly related branches, especially in the separation of Thymallinae (grayling species), Coregoninae (whitefishes such as powan and schelly) and the Salmoninae (various species of trout charr and salmon). There is a much wider disparity of opinion when it comes to the classification of closer relatives, especially within the charrs and whitefishes. There is a whole section of fisheries research dedicated to resolving this issue and much remains to be clarified. Personally I have found the work of Professor Eugenia Dorofeya of the Russian Academy of Sciences, encapsulating both her own studies and those of other scientists, most helpful in developing a strategic viewpoint. The dendograms she presented to the 6th International Workshop of the International Society of Arctic Charr Fanatics at Murmansk in 1990 are reproduced in figure 1.

Ferox, being a variety of trout, belong, together with the Atlantic and Pacific salmon species and the charrs, to the sub-family Salmoninae of the family Salmonidae. The three main groupings within this sub-family apparently had their evolutionary origins in three distinct major sea basins. The charrs, including our own native species *Salvelinus alpinus* L., were derived from ancestral stock living in the Arctic sea basin. Brown trout (*Salmo trutta* L.,) and the Atlantic salmon (*Salmo salar* L.), together with the genus *Salmothymus*, originated in the Atlantic. The various members of the genus Oncorhynchus, which includes the rainbow trout *Oncorhynchus mykiss,* (previously wrongly placed in the genus *Salmo*), and its near relatives the Pacific salmon species originated from a common ancestor inhabiting the Pacific. The fact that we use the terms Arctic charr, Atlantic salmon and Pacific salmon in the first place is in part a subconscious recognition of this large-scale geographical sub-division in these branches of the family tree. It is comparatively easy on this grand geographical scale to grasp the likely effects of distance and time in allowing divergence from a common ancestral fish species into the ones we recognise today. However it is important also to comprehend that shorter periods of time and smaller distances of geographical isolation can have fundamental effects on the evolution of a single species of fish. These are the more subtle manifestations of genetic change described, depending on the author, as a sub-species, race, variety, etc. Here again in the case of the northern fish species we have to look to glacial periodicity as a major causative agent aided and abetted of course by the well-known strong homing instinct of salmonid fish to their spawning grounds.

In the process of glaciation large amounts of the Earth's water are locked up in the form of ice or snow. This causes a substantial drop in sea level, during which new, separate sea basins are formed. The ancestors of our present stocks of trout salmon and charr were sea-going, running into fresh water to spawn and also developing permanent resident freshwater populations where conditions allowed. Charr in the British Isles have, in

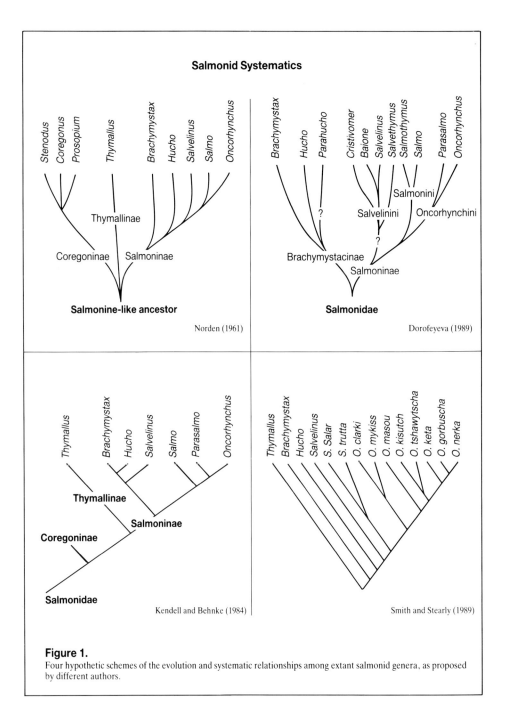

Figure 1.
Four hypothetic schemes of the evolution and systematic relationships among extant salmonid genera, as proposed by different authors.

the current climatic conditions, lost this sea-going habit. The waxing and the waning of the glaciers created conditions where stocks of fish could be separated from each other for many thousands of years, only to be brought back together as the ice retreated or glacial ice dams caused water levels to transcend previously distinct watersheds. The separation and mixing of stocks could operate over both small and large distances, only once, on many occasions and on numerous time-scales within the glacial period. To us the glacial periods lasted an immensely long time, but on the time-scale of the history of the Earth they occupied a mere moment of geological time; too short, often, for a clear-cut differentiation of fish stocks into easily defined main groupings that we can readily recognise in the major sea basins of the world today, but long enough to present our classification system with a major challenge in defining the plethora of forms of charr trout and whitefishes that now occupy the recently deglaciated areas of Eurasia and North America. We also have to take into account the ten to twelve thousand years or so of the current inter-glacial period in creating further opportunities for populations of fish to continue to evolve differences between stocks within each individual river or loch system, and of course from fish populations in other watersheds.

It is a problem shared with, but not necessarily halved by, workers in other environmental disciplines. As someone with a passion for trees that rivals that which I have for Ferox and charr, I am aware that my colleagues in the silvicultural field have similar problems in trying to encompass the diversity of forms exhibited in single species of willow, birch and alder. The giant evolutionary 'experiment' initiated by the Ice Age has thrown up much to confound and challenge us, including the origins of modern man and his relation to our Neanderthal relatives. We will never get to meet a Neanderthal man and ask him what he thinks of the sporting and culinary qualities of Ferox, his Ice Age companion. However we can still encounter this special form of trout and others too. When we do, we should pause and ponder a moment on this confusing and beautiful example of evolutionary diversity and appreciate its link with our own glacial past.

Individual variation is normal in most animal species. We see this every day in common animals such as ourselves and accommodate it within our overall internal picture of the world without any conscious effort. We can also detect, without going into detailed statistical and genetic analyses, that groups of individuals within the people we meet every day are more like each other than the general population, i.e. they have family characteristics. We also recognise major differences between groups of people who inhabit different areas of the world, i.e. they have racial characteristics. This is part of the biological reality of variation in the human species, regardless of the views of extremists, with which we have to live. It is much the same in other species including trout and resolving the individual, group and population characteristics within the species we have come to accept – for the time being perhaps as *Salmo trutta* L. – into a definitive, generally acceptable schematic framework is a task as yet incomplete.

Any experienced trout angler is well aware of the richness of individual variation in the fish he or she catches. Indeed the beauty of the animal, especially in its colour and spot pattern variation is one of the intrinsic qualities of the angling experience itself. Practitioners of the sport quickly appreciate the substantial differences in form and colour, not only between individual fish from one water body, but also from different types of loch, lake or river. This variation is apparently not random. Certain consistencies are obvious even to the casual observer, e.g. between trout from peaty hill tarns and those from clear lowland rivers. In large natural water bodies anglers have long discerned certain common group characteristics in catches of fish from different parts of the loch or lake and have assigned to them special names. Professional fish biologists dare not scoff at such 'cracker barrel' classifications with the now famous case of Lough Melvin there to chide them. Here the research of Professor Andrew Ferguson of Queen's University, Belfast into the genetic relationship of the various groups of trout subjectively classified by local anglers as Gillaroo, Sonaghen and Ferox thoroughly vindicated the angler's choice of sub-division. This does not mean to say of course that this will be exactly the same case in every water apparently containing multiple forms of trout, but some kind of biological consistency seems to exist and is being further investigated. The phenomenon is widely recognised in Scandinavia and Europe and it appears likely that similar sub-divisions exist in Highland lochs such as Rannoch, Earn and Morar.

However, this search for a rationalisation of the consistency in variation of the myriad colour and body forms of trout is not new by any means. It is something that has captivated angler and biologist alike for centuries, especially in the great age of classification and collection of the eighteenth and nineteenth centuries. There is much to admire in the way the great naturalists and angler-naturalists of this period dealt with the difficult task of trying to render order out of the large diversity of trout found in the British Isles and elsewhere. Reading the works of the Reverend Houghton, Frank Buckland, Jonathan Couch, Dr Gunther and Francis Day etc. is a pleasure in itself, and likewise with the twentieth century contributions of Tate Regan, R. P. Hardie and Dr Niall Campbell. Anyone seriously interested in Ferox should add these works to their reading list and make additions to it from the excellent set of other references they make. All of these above-mentioned authors cite Ferox to a greater or lesser degree in their works, and their writings reveal the still unresolved dichotomy of viewpoint regarding the genetic distinction of Ferox from other trout. None deny the special interest that such a large piscivorous fish generates. We should remember that these early workers were without the benefit of the modern techniques of electrophoretic and DNA analyses. The fact that these modern scientific methods have vindicated some of their findings is a testimony to their observational and recording skills.

John Berkenhout (1789) is generally given credit for categorising the 'Great Lake Trout' as a special form of trout. It is important of course to realise that he was talking about the European species. The North American 'Lake Trout' is actually a species of charr! His description of the former is curt yet sums up some of the essential features of Ferox 'lake trout. Sometimes fifty to sixty pounds. Probably a distinct species. In the north.' Sir William Jardine (1835), however coined the specific appellation 'Ferox' that has borne the vicissitudes of time and scientific fashion to this day and given us the emotive name that conjures up the passion and fire that drives anglers and scientists to pursue and study it.

Jardine was a keen angler himself, and I for one am willing to believe that he knew what he was doing when he gave the fish such an evocative name. Thankfully he did, and I would not in the least grudge him this minor form of immortality. The old Norse expression 'word fame' is very apt here. Say 'Ferox' even slightly louder than normal in an angler-frequented pub and most likely you will be the subject of quizzical glances. Your conversation will perhaps be eavesdropped, albeit politely, and people will find an excuse to start up a chat with you at the bar. You may even, if your day has been successful, be gifted a wee dram! 'What's in a name?' is certainly not just a rhetorical question in this instance. For anglers besotted with their capture it is probably a form of obsessive 'mental illness'. For me it is a lifelong fascination both as a sportsman and scientist. For our predecessors in both fields, especially in the Victorian and Edwardian eras it was a challenge to their desire to have the natural world classified in an ordered fashion.

In forming their definition and describing the characteristics of Ferox, the chroniclers of earlier times had to rely on measurements of the body proportions of internal and external features of the fish. They then had to summarise their results as they stood in relation to the characteristics of other types of trout. This form of analysis is known to scientists as morphometric or meristic analysis and is still a very useful tool today. The system has, like others, its own particular drawbacks, especially in this case the fact that some of the physical features of fish are affected by their environment and are highly variable. In coming to conclusions about the taxonomic position of the fish being studied this has to be carefully borne in mind.

The overall validity of the techniques, despite certain caveats, is not in question and it has certainly played its part in determining the special place of Ferox in our overview of the status of various forms of trout and, more especially, of charr. Modern statistical analyses and powerful computer programs render the monumental task faced by the scientists of yesteryear of collating and processing the data collected as relative childs play'.

More recently, advances in biochemical and cellular biological studies have allowed scientists to say more about the fixed genetic characteristics of various forms of charr and trout, including Ferox. These 'genetic finger-printing' methods are certainly helping to elucidate the special nature of the beast. The validation of the separation of the trout of Lough Melvin into Gillaroo, Sonaghen and Ferox by Professor Ferguson is a shining example. Dr Alistair Stephen, chairman of the Ferox 85 Group, carried out similar electrophoretic research into the status of Scottish Ferox in a number of different locations. This did not completely agree with the clear-cut example of Lough Melvin and further research is ongoing. In this, myself and other members of the Ferox 85 Group are providing support to Professor Ferguson in the provision of further samples from Scotland. We await the results with avid anticipation. My personal view is that a strong genetic distinction, probably initiated at the beginning of the last glaciation, will also be found between Ferox and other forms of trout in Highland lochs. I would also predict differences between Ferox in different watersheds, and that some lochs will have more than one race of Ferox.

Whatever the matrix of morphometric data throws up, or the delicacies of DNA analysis delineates, there is another, more empirical means of testing the inherited propensities of Ferox. It is again one that has a close analogue in the science of silviculture. Foresters have long conducted field trials in different regional origins with the same tree species. This has shown a wide range of performance in growth, form and survival in the various seed sources. This is of major economic importance and not just an esoteric exercise for the hobby botanist. Whatever one feels about the large-scale conifer plantations of recent years in upland Britain (personally I detest them), foresters have shown a great deal of expertise in matching seed origins from abroad to the local soil/site conditions. I have found that such foresters readily appreciate that different origins of fish might have fixed genetic features that would maintain differential performance in survival and growth even when transferred to new locations. Such studies on provenance – or more correctly origin trials – have never been part of a systematic study of Ferox populations in Britain. In the nearest European country to the Scottish Highlands, Norway, such trials have in fact taken place. This is of particular interest as many of the geological, climatic and ecological conditions of the Scottish Highlands are in some ways closer to southern Norway than to the rest of the British Isles.

Some twenty-odd years ago I had the good fortune to be invited to Norway by Professor Per Aass to participate in his work on charr and trout at Lake Tunhovdfjord. Professor Aass has been involved for several

Catching adult ferox for egg collection, Lake Tunhovdfjord. (*Per Aass*)

decades in research on this freshwater lake (in southern Norway 'fjord' is also used to describe a long narrow freshwater body much in the same way as Scots use 'loch' to describe both sea and freshwater bodies). His main research interests included much work on the sporting and commercial fisheries for charr. In its main physical and chemical parameters Lake Tunhovd has much in common with lochs such as Rannoch. The combined fisheries for charr at Lake Tunhovd produce annually a yield of five to ten metric tonnes comprising tens of thousands of individual fish. This in turn has made available to Per and his monitoring team a vast database on the biology of the charr population. This was the main motivation for my study trip and it greatly assisted me in my approach to the study of charr in Scotland. For that I owe Per and his colleagues my eternal gratitude.

The visit to Tunhovd had another important impact on me that also affected my whole outlook on my angling and professional life – the sight of its incredible Ferox. The first wild trout I saw in Norway was a magnificent hen fish of 24lb, and the next a cock fish of some 19lb. Yet these are comparative tiddlers compared to the 30- and 35lb monsters recorded in recent years. These two fish – especially the hen – gave the lie to the often expressed accusations of ugliness levelled at Ferox by some anglers in Britain. Tunhovd Ferox are the subject of much interest in Norway and their progeny are in high demand for stocking trials. Per Aass has, apart from his work with this strain of fish in its own locale, carried out a number of stock origin trials, reminiscent of those of the silviculturalist, with Ferox from this lake and other lakes and with other forms of trout. The performance of the various origins of trout were clearly different. Tunhovd Ferox outper-formed several other trout strains when introduced to other mountain charr lakes. In one lake where the local trout did not eat charr, the Tunhovd race accessed this food source and quickly attained larger sizes than any earlier recorded in the local native trout. However, Tunhovd Ferox did not perform as well in large lowland lakes such as Lake Mjøsa in southern Norway, where, due to the absence of charr, the main prey of the local Ferox consists of whitefish species such as powan and smelt. This in itself is interesting, but when the results of reciprocal stocking of Ferox from lowland 'whitefish' lakes showed the reverse was also true, one is entitled to consider that once you have seen one Ferox you have certainly not seen them all. It is difficult to be certain about why these origin trials showed up the differences they exhibited. The physical and biological environments the various Ferox strains came from are obviously an important factor especially in the range of prey species available.

The link of predator to prey is a complex one and it is often difficult to separate both cause and effect and 'top down' and 'bottom up' interactions. Fish are not cogent or sapient in maximising their metabolic processes in their battle for survival. As long as they are satisfying their energy and protein requirements they care little for the scientists trying to decipher their life history strategies. However, it is clear that both the prey species present and its/their age and growth characteristics are of primary importance in providing the opportunity for a population of Ferox to flourish. In Britain this opportunity is mainly provided by Arctic charr and it is common parlance these days to mention Ferox and charr in the same breath. This is no doubt due in large part to classic works such as Hardie's (1940), and the more recent works of Dr Niall Campbell (1979). Although we tend to take the predator/prey relationship of Ferox and charr in Scotland for granted, it was not until Dr Campbell's work was published that definitive data and references on the presence of charr in the stomachs of Scottish Ferox was available. This is strange indeed perhaps considering the well-known examples from Scandinavia, Ireland and the English Lake District. Much of the data on the occurrence of charr in Ferox stomachs presented in Dr Campbell's summary was derived from some of my own studies in a number of Scottish lochs. Since his work was published, thanks to the efforts of friends and colleagues in the Ferox 85 Group this database has expanded considerably and has generally confirmed the importance of charr in the diet of Scottish Ferox. It has also further supported the impression that a prey fish of around one third of the length of the Ferox is the preferred option, though larger and smaller fish do feature, including other prey species. More extensive studies in Norwegian and Swedish charr/trout lakes solidly support this and further justify the image of the voraciousness of Ferox in the minds of anglers. For many years however there has never been any doubt in my mind about this particular characteristic of Ferox. After seeing that the above-mentioned 19lb Norwegian Ferox had nine 6oz charr in its stomach, and once finding in the stomach of a Ferox from the Gaick district of Inverness-shire a trout half its own length, there was no

PREY-FISH SIZE IN STOMACHS OF HIGHLAND FEROX

Ferox Length(cm)	Prey Length(cm)	Loch	Data Source
72.0	18.5, 12.0	Arkaig	Ferox 85 Group
81.5	19.5, 20.0	Arkaig	Ferox 85 Group
48.5	7.0	Arkaig	Ferox 85 Group
84.0	28.0	Arkaig	Campbell(1979)
49.0	25.0, 12.0	An t Seilich	Campbell(1979)
38.0	12.0	An t Seilich	Campbell(1979)
55.0	13.0, 8.0	Rannoch	Ferox 85 Group
48.0	22.0	Rannoch	Ferox 85 Group
64.7	19.1	Rannoch	Campbell(1979)
38.5	13.5	Ness	Campbell(1979)
69.0	21.5	Ness	Campbell(1979)
27.0	4.0	Cuaich	Campbell(1979)
22.0	6.0	Cuaich	Campbell(1979)
57.0	20.0	Garry(Inverness)	Campbell(1979)
40.0	10.3	Veyatie	Campbell(1979)
47.0	16.0	Garry(Perth)	SOAFD Pitlochry
30.5	10.0-11.0	Garry(Perth)	SOAFD Pitlochry
30.0	10.0	Garry(Perth	SOAFD Pitlochry
28.5	9.5,10	Garry(Perth)	SOAFD Pitlochry

room for dubiety as to what they are capable of. This information once helped to provide the rather flippant response from me, 'anything it bloody-well likes' when questioned about what a Ferox eats. Not too much of an exaggeration if you have seen Ferox 'rising' to consume lemmings on their suicidal journey to oblivion in Norwegian lakes, or found rodents in the stomachs of Ferox from Scottish lochs. These rather 'exotic' items aside, the main prey of Ferox in glacial ribbon lakes is likely to be the main species of fish occupying the mid- and open water areas (pelagic zone). In the British situation this most frequently happens to be charr; it may very occasionally be powan or pollan. In Scandinavian lakes it may be a number of combinations or single populations of charr, powan, cisco, vendace or smelt. It may even be the case that if none of the above species is present, and the role of the harvester of 'water fleas' is taken up by a specialised race of plankton-feeding trout, that Ferox are exclusively cannibalistic. The most widely-known case of this type in Norway is in Lake Jølster where, in the absence of charr, their role is taken up by a charr-like race of trout. I would not be surprised if this is also the case in Loch Laidon, a renowned Ferox water to the west of Loch Rannoch. I would like to make a plea to the reader not to embrace the term 'cannibal trout' in the usual pejorative sense with which it is often used in ill-informed descriptions of Ferox. Of course Ferox do eat other trout, there is no doubt about it, but pike eat other pike and salmon parr will eat the eggs of adult salmon yet it is ferox that get the bad name. Not that Ferox really care about human prejudices of course, and in addition to their main diet they will happily devour frogs, newts, rodents, migrating salmon smolts and most probably the 'dumbo' escapees from the rainbow trout and smolt-rearing cages that now in my opinion, blight the visual amenity and environmental integrity of Highland lochs.

We should also not take the noble image of Ferox as a magnificent predator of nimble, dashing shoals of charr as an all-defining one. They are of course active predators on healthy living fish, but they will also turn readily to scavenging; in the world of an energy-demanding predator an easy meal is not to be missed. The 'king of beasts' itself, the lion, is not averse to stealing the kills of lesser hunters. Pike are well-known scavengers. The sporting gentlemen of yesteryear, such as Osgood MacKenzie, mention the successful use of dead-baiting for Ferox especially at night. It is a method that I and my friends have put to good effect ourselves.

We are only now beginning to understand the influence of species and population structure of potential prey species on the development of our British Ferox populations. Dr Campbell's work has indicated a switch from an insect-eating diet to a fish diet when potential Ferox reach a length of around thirty to thirty-five centimetres. Thereafter they seem mainly to prey on charr about a third of their own length. This strong and clear relationship between the length of predator and prey has been also noted in Norwegian charr and powan lakes. However, the age and growth structure of these populations is critical for the Ferox. Twenty years ago my Norwegian colleague, Dr Per Aass, pointed out to me that Ferox were unlikely to be present in lakes where the potential prey fish consisted of relatively few, fast-growing fish that quickly attained lengths much in excess of thirty centimetres. The most suitable scenario for Ferox was a situation where the prey fish population consisted of a large number of relatively slow-growing individuals, say from 'fingerling size' to 'herring size'. This criterion seems to be well met in the age and growth structure of the charr populations of several well-known Ferox lochs of the Highlands (see figure 2). Knowing the preferred prey size selection of Ferox, from the back-calculated growth from scale readings of individual fish and the linking of this with the known age/length data on the charr concerned, it is possible to postulate that once a potential Ferox has reached the critical length suggested by Dr Campbell for changing to a fish diet its subsequent growth and feeding patterns are very closely tied in with the various year classes of charr. The age class structure and therefore the relative abundance of potential, ideally sized prey items may explain why waters like Loch Laggan and Loch Garry with few charr over twenty-five centimetres appear to produce very few Ferox in excess of 10lb, whereas waters such as Loch Rannoch, where charr over twenty-five centimetres are apparently more abundant, have a pedigree of producing double figure Ferox. This should be taken as an indication only and more research is obviously required, but the close two-way intimacy of predator and prey has to be kept in mind. Further elucidation on this is provided by the works of the Norwegian scientists in examining the diet of Ferox and their role in the ecosystem. Of particular interest are the studies of Jostein Skurdal, Ola Hegge and Trond Taugbøl in the lakes Mjøsa, Randsfjord and Tyrifjord and the investigations of Odd Terje and Tor Naesje using data not only from these lakes but also other Norwegian Ferox waters such as Lake Femund.

Length Relationship between Brown Trout (Ferox predator) and Charr (prey) in Loch Ness

Month	No.	Length (cm)	Weight (g)	Sex	Prey Length (extrapolated where necessary)	% of Predator body length
July	5	47.4	1016.6	F	13.0	27.4
Aug	14	38.7	650	M	11.0	28.4
	15	46.0	1045		14.5	31.5
	"	"	"		15.5	33.7
Oct	21	26.7	194.5	F	3.5	13.1
	30	29.5	308.4		5.6	19.0
	34	35.2	471.9	F	8.0	22.7
	35	34.7	501.6	F	9.0	25.9
	36	35.5	507.8	F	11.3	31.8
	"	"	"	"	7.1	20.0
	"	"	"	"	6.6	18.6
	38	40.6	715.1		5.5	13.5
	39	45.5	936.5		4.0	8.8
	"	"	"		4.0	8.8
	40	46.7	1020		14.6	31.3
	43	52.4	1674.5		10.8	20.6
	44	57.9	2033.5	F	21.5	37.1
	"	"	"	"	12.3	21.2

From Martin & Shine (1994)

In Norwegian Ferox waters it is a general rule of thumb that Ferox switch from an invertebrate diet to a fish diet at a length of twenty to twenty-five centimetres. This is somewhat smaller than in the known case of our own

The impressive maw of a 'double figure' ferox. The last thing its prey sees! (*A. Stephen*)

Ferox. This may be a function of the population and species structure of the potential prey species available, but Dr Campbell did mention in his work that there was some evidence to suggest that Ferox in Scottish lochs started to switch to fish feeding at below thirty centimetres. Personally I think this may be the case in many of our waters, and probably the difference between the Scottish and Norwegian situation is mainly a function of the greater database in Norway. The Norwegians appear to hold their Ferox in higher regard than we do. Perhaps it is time we changed this.

The ideal situation for the 'new' Ferox entrant to encounter is to find an abundant prey population that consists of slow-growing individuals with a low size at adult sexual maturity. Such is the situation with charr in many Scottish hydro-electric reservoirs, but in Scandinavia the opportunities are more complex owing to the wider distribution of other alternative prey species. Smelt (*Osmerus eperlanus*) or sparling as they are usually called in Scotland, are found as permanent inhabitants in many Scandinavian freshwater lakes and exist in vast numbers. They form the main prey of Ferox and landlocked salmon in Lake Vänern in Sweden and are the main food source of Ferox in Lake Mjøsa. The mature adult size of these smelt is normally ten to twelve centimetres.

In places like Mjøsa with a very high density of smelt of several year classes (830 fish per hectare) all age groups of smelt are preyed upon by Ferox and there is no strong relationship between prey size and predator

Size of Prey in Ferox Stomachs from Lake Tyrifjord

Ferox Length(cm)	No Examined	Mean Prey Length(cm)
30-39	2	10
40-49	7	13
50-59	1	13
60-69	6	29
70-79	27	28
80-89	36	29
90-96	4	28

[1]based on Skurdal et al.1992

size as there often is in charr and powan waters. There is a trade-off going on between the energy needed to capture prey and the energy obtained from eating it. A large prey gives more back, but it is more difficult to capture; small fish give less but are easier to obtain. In Mjøsa, even though there are other potentially larger prey fish such as powan, the density of smelt is sufficiently high to make it more worthwhile for the Ferox to concentrate on the smelt. Smelt comprise almost ninety per cent of the diet

% Composition of Prey Fish in Ferox from Two Norwegian Lakes

Lake	Powan	Cisco	Charr	Burbot	Smelt	Sample
Femund	58	n/a	32	10	n/a	74
Mjosa	1	4	n/a	0	95	250

[1]based on Sandlund and Naesje .1984

of Ferox here. In lake Randsfjord smelt comprise more than fifty per cent of the diet of Ferox. Prey density here is also quite high (770 fish per hectare) and once again there is little correlation between prey and predator size. All age/length groups of smelt are capable of being consumed by trout over twenty-five to thirty centimetres in length. The situation in Lake Tyrifjord was very different. Prey fish densities were much lower than at the first two lakes (345 fish per hectare) and the response of Ferox to this situation varied accordingly. Smelt comprised twelve per cent of their diet and powan about fifty per cent. Other significant prey species were charr, perch, sticklebacks and minnows. The trade-off here was for the Ferox initially to exploit smelt until they attained a length of sixty centimetres, at which point they switched to the larger powan. In this sense they were repeating the energy-driven changes of their earlier diet switch from invertebrates. A clear relationship between prey and predator size was also noted in Femund. Here Ferox preferentially preyed on powan between five and eighteen centimetres in length; charr between five and eighteen centimetres and burbot (*Lota lota* L.) between eight and twelve. The top down effect of the Ferox on the prey fish in these examples is very different. In the case of smelt, where the adult mature size is less than fifteen centimetres and all age groups are consumed by Ferox, predation mortality is spread across the population. In the other species predation mortality is focused on the younger age groups.

Ferox Prey Densities in 3 Norwegian Lakes[1]

Lake	No fish/ha	% over 20cm
Mjosa	833	8.5
Tyrifjord	345	27.5
Randsfjord	770	19.0

[1]based on Skurda et al 1992

The ramifications of this work, apart from the envy I feel as a scientist who would like to be funded to carry out similar work, is immense. What is the differential (if any) between the Ferox-induced mortality of the Rannoch benthic and pelagic charr in the various age and size classes? Do Ferox in Loch Awe move up the grade to charr and trout after feeding on salmon smolts or perch fry? Can we manipulate the prey populations to favour Ferox? Only time and a major cash injection into research will tell. The Scandinavian analogy is very worthwhile, and as a Nordophile I like making it. I would much prefer though to get the primary information from our own waters.

Regardless of whether the main prey is charr, powan or smelt, or of where and how the Ferox elects to catch them it is that initial switch from a diet of predominately invertebrate animals (snails, shrimps, insect larvae etc.) to one mainly consisting of fish that facilitates the remarkable increase

The bony parts of 23lb ferox's jaws are well equipped to deal with catching fish. (*David Hay*)

of growth that makes Ferox what they are to the angler. Depending on each individual situation, any potential Ferox may have to wait a considerable time, sometimes up to a third of its life-span, before it reaches the critical size altering it easily to catch young charr or other prey fish. The fact that it can 'afford to' is due to a feature of the biology of fish that is very different from mammals such as ourselves. Fish, unlike warm-blooded creatures such as humans, can continue to grow throughout their entire lives. The insect-eating phase of a Ferox's life can be considered as a form of apprenticeship through which they pass on their way to becoming the 'behemoth' we all seek. It can be a difficult apprenticeship however, and a substantial proportion of the young fish that enter the 'trade' of charr-killer never make it through the rites of passage to piscivorous journeyman. They perish with the other strains of trout which generally attain lesser life-spans. Those fish who pass through this difficult transition are rewarded very well as they seek to meet their energy and protein requirements. Individual fish can double their weight in their first Ferox season, and even at much later stages in life can make very substantial gains in body weight. From a known length–weight relationship and knowledge of back-calculated length determined from scale readings, it was estimated that a 22lb Ferox from Loch Awe had put on an increment of 4lb in its final season. Another fish from the same loch had attained a weight of 23lb at the early age of six years. Clearly, compared to the time they spend as an invertebrate predator, life as a fish consumer is a piece of cake for Ferox. The only reason for these fish attaining the remarkable growth and size that they do is because they are meeting their energy and protein requirements very easily. Yet there are still those who regard Ferox as inefficient predators! This is palpably not the case. Ferox have been a feature of our upland waters since the cessation of the last Ice Age, and probably existed well before it. They have survived the passage of time very well indeed for a 'failure'.

Ferox are prodigious consumers of prey fish such as charr, capturing and eating, according to my colleague Dr Niall Campbell, up to fifteen per cent of their total body weight in a single feeding session. The total annual consumption of charr by piscivorous trout in Lake Tunhovd was estimated by my Norwegian colleague Professor Per Aass to be around four kilograms

A partially digested charr 'robbed' from a ferox about 6lb when the rapala (13cm) hooked the meal rather than the predator. (*Alistair Thorne*)

per hectare. In this lake a substantial gill-net and angling harvest of charr exists, yielding annual rates in the order of two to three kilograms of char per hectare, therefore providing several metric tons of charr each year to the commercial and recreational fishermen. Thus the Ferox here seem to be outdoing their human counterparts. Using the food conversion rate of consumed charr to Ferox flesh of 7:1 suggested by Dr Campbell in his 1979 paper, together with the information from the above Norwegian case, we can infer that in a 2,000 hectare lake more than a ton of Ferox flesh is being maintained in such situations. Professor Aass is less generous in the estimated conversion rate of charr to Ferox at 10:1, but this still leaves the possibility that more than 10 metric tonnes of charr are being consumed each year in Lake Tunhovd. Perhaps as much as 1.5 tonnes of charr-eating trout are being maintained annually on this basis in Tunhovd.

The definitive age and size structure of individual Ferox populations are still not clear and much research remains necessary before we can make authoritative statements about how many Ferox exist in any given water; however, in our larger waters we are probably talking about hundreds of individual fish. The concept of Ferox being very rare is not a viewpoint I can share. Whilst we obviously cannot expect a top predator such as Ferox to be the most common fish in the water, there is probably no cause for concern about population sizes in the relatively unexploited lochs of the Scottish Highlands. However, in lakes such as Windermere whose environmental integrity has been compromised by pollution and nutrient enrichment, where the components of the fish community have been altered by introductions by man, and where the changed conditions favour species other than charr and trout, then there may be some cause for concern. Similar concerns may also be justified in some of the loughs of Ireland and Scotland after the thoughtless introduction of exotic species such as pike and ruffe.

The evolutionary position of Ferox,their ecology and their fish-eating propensities no doubt stir some interest in the heart of the serious angler as well as the naturalist. However, when considering what really makes an angler burn, when thinking about Ferox, one would have to admit that size is the single most important factor. This is not to deny quality and beauty too of course, but the thought of a huge wild trout testing out your tackle is the real attraction. Legendary long-ago leviathans probably feature in the 'public bar mythology' of Ferox as much as they do in the lore of pike anglers, and a fine thing too! The reality is of course rather different, but there is yet sufficient meat on the myth to keep even the most cynical happy.

Whether we can take the statement of Berkenhout (1789) of the Great Lake trout of European waters reaching weights of 50 or 60lb seriously is open to question. Even the Reverend Houghton in his quotation (1879) of the above author places a question mark alongside in brackets. Yet this is perhaps unkind, as definitive records of 50lb trout do indeed exist. Tate Regan (1911) mentions that trout over 30lb used to be quite common in Lough Neagh in Ulster and that trout as heavy as 50lb have been reported here. We cannot deny that such prodigious proportions can be reached by wild trout. Scientifically ratified weights of trout up to 25½ kilograms (56lb) have been recorded from Lake Lokvara in the former Yugoslav Republic. Neither this record nor indeed the huge trout of Lough Neagh may meet the definition of Dr Niall Campbell or that used by the Ferox 85 Group of a true Ferox. This could even apply to the previous world rod-caught record of 16.3 kilograms (35.8lb) mentioned by Peter Maitland and Niall Campbell in

WEIGHT lbs	SITE	CAPTOR	YEAR	BAIT/LURE
10	Arkaig	R Greer	1986	wobbled trout
10	Laggan	A McMorrine	1992	Rapala
10 2oz	Laggan	B Macauslan	1990	Rapala
11 4oz	Arkaig	R Greer	1985	wobbled trout
12	Rannoch	R Greer	1990	wobbled trout
12 8oz	Rannoch	MGreenhalgh	1992	Rapala
12 8oz	Rannoch	R Greer	1994	Rapala
14	Rannoch	I Pirnie	1991	spun trout
15	Rannoch	S Thorne	1994	Rapala
15	Rannoch	R Greer	1992	wobbled charr
16	Rannoch	I Pirnie	1990	spun finnock
17	Arkaig	I Pirnie	1989	wobbled charr
19 10.4oz	Awe	A Thorne	1993	wobbled trout

their book *Freshwater Fishes* (1992). This remarkable fish caught by an Argentinean, Eugenio Cavaglia, was replaced on the record books by a true Ferox caught by the Swede Kurt Stenlund of Malmberget in northern Sweden. Herr Stenlund's massive fish weighed in at 17 kilograms (37½lb) and at a length of 105 centimetres (three feet five inches). His achievement was part of an established Swedish 'tradition' of producing huge brown trout. The Swedish *Fishing Times* in 1956 reported two of the largest legitimately recorded trout in Sweden. These came from Lake Vättern and weighed in at 16.4 kilograms (36.1lb) and 18 kilograms (39.6lb). However, these are just tiddlers compared to a 23 kilograms (50.6lb) trout reported from the same lake.

Lake Mjøsa, the largest and deepest lake in Norway, rivals the record of Vattern in producing giant trout. Mjøsa in fact occupies a premier position in the pantheon of piscatorial fame. In 1963, rod-caught fish of 12.6 kilograms (27.7lb) and 13 kilograms (28.6lb) were reported in the angling press, but even these pale beside a Ferox of 18 kilograms (39.6lb) and 104 centimetres (three feet four inches) recorded by Dr Hiutfield Kaas in 1938. And even this Mjøsa monster is surpassed by earlier giants of 22 kilograms (48.4lb) and 23 kilograms (50.6lb). Other Norwegian waters such as Lake Tyrifjord, Lake Randsfjord and Lake Tunhovdfjord are known to produce Ferox between 10-15 kilograms (22 to 33lb). Fennoscandian Ferox waters should be on the itinerary of all dedicated to the capture of high quality wild trout. Their potential is perhaps rivalled by the Alpine lakes of Austria and Switzerland, though in modern times pollution and abstraction has robbed them of some of their former glories, and what glories they were. For example, Menzies (1936) reported trout of 42-, 45- and 47lb from the Traum

See in the mountains of Austria. He also mentions a trout of 44lb from the Lunzer See and two fish of 39lb from both Lake Lugano and Vilalpsee. These huge Continental and Scandinavian fish are a mere sample and more could be cited, but it is time to consider our own backyard.

In my opinion, wild trout of over 30lb are well within the realms of reality for any angler willing to take up the pursuit of Ferox in the British Isles; it is only a few thousand rod hours of carefully thought out effort away for the truly relentless. Speaking mainly as an angler I believe that there is sufficient historical, anecdotal and biological evidence to support this contention. While it is true that the current rod-caught record of Alistair Thorne of the Ferox 85 Group is below the magical 20lb barrier, this in no way approaches the biological limit for the species, as we can see from the above overseas examples. His record also reflects the nature of tighter recording protocols that operate today, and which now exclude the records of past angling eras. Justifiable and highly laudable as these protocols are, we should not let them obscure or deny the achievement of the capture of large Ferox by our predecessors. Regrettably, the erstwhile world record rod-caught record trout of 39½lb from Loch Awe, taken by Mr W. Muir in 1866, has not stood the test of time. Recently I have been in correspondence

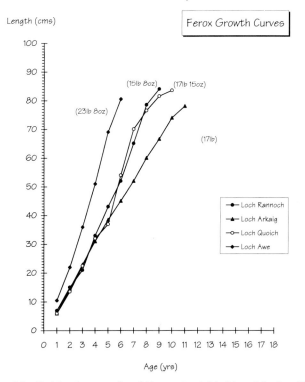

Examples of individual growth of Ferox in 4 highland lochs. These fish are not necessarily typical of the whole population!

with one of his descendants, Lt-Colonel P.B. Peyman, who maintains a strong interest in his ancestor's great achievement. Lt-Colonel Peyman has been in touch with the International Game Fish Association and the *Guinness Book of Records* to ascertain the reason why the 'Great Loch Awe Fish' was removed from the lists. The fish was taken on a trolled fly, but this was not embedded in the inside of the jaw and therefore it was considered to have been foul-hooked. Some doubt has been expressed by authors such as Menzies (1936) that many large Ferox of the past were salmon mistaken as trout. There is no direct allegation that the Loch Awe fish was a salmon and we should not simply deny its validity because of its large size. Mr Muir and his ghillie Nicol McIntyre were seasoned campaigners who caught both salmon and trout and knew well the difference between the species. The giant trout in its glass case was kept in family possession for fifty years until, in one of those twists of fate that make legends what they are, it was destroyed in a house fire in 1912. Modern techniques of DNA fingerprinting could otherwise have settled the issue beyond doubt, and I think would have proved Lt-Colonel Peyman's point. In my heart this is the record I wish to break however often fruitless days break my heart.

The pedigree of Loch Awe in producing potential pretenders to the throne of Ferox is not in question. Some years ago my colleague Ian Hynd

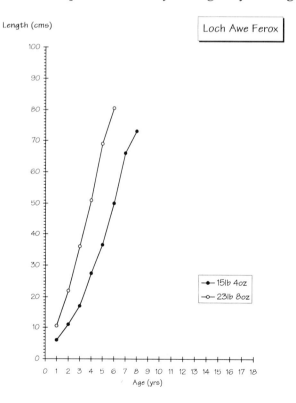

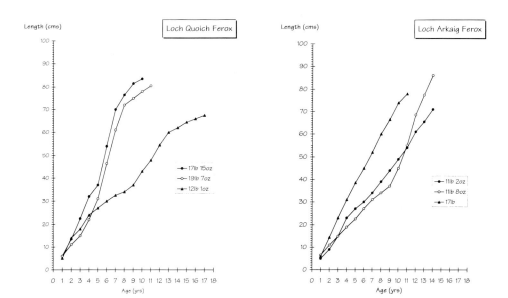

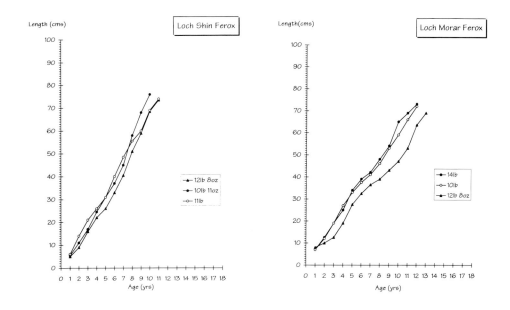

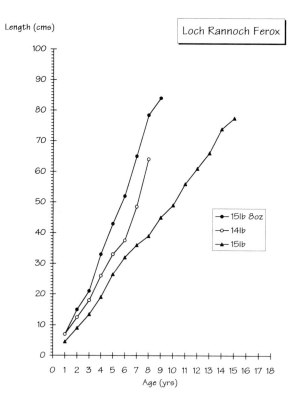

and I made an *ad hoc* coffee-break comparison of growth rates of some Norwegian and Scottish Ferox. This showed that Loch Awe Ferox grew much faster than the Ferox of Tunhovdfjord, which are known to exceed 30lb. The Loch Awe Ferox were in fact very similar in growth rate to the Lake Mjøsa Ferox. There is no biological reason that I know of which would preclude a 40lb Ferox coming from Loch Awe. However, definitive records of fish over 20lb from Loch Awe are rare; Sir John Colqhoun of Luss mentioning only one, though T. Stoddart in his book *The Art of Angling as Practised in Scotland* (1835) mentions a Mr Maule who was reputed to have caught trout up to 27lb

Loch Rannoch, on the other hand, has several 'twenty pounders' to its credit, including a 21lb fish caught by Major Cheape in 1849; a 22lb fish taken by Mr F. Twist in 1867, and a 21lb fish caught by Miss K .H. Kirby in 1904. Malloch (1910) presents photographs of several double figure fish from Rannoch including a 19lb specimen. These fish are dwarfed however by a 30lb Ferox reported by Stoddart (1835) to have been caught by Baron Norton in 1800. Rannoch should therefore feature prominently in the Ferox fisher's diary, and it is no coincidence that the Ferox-85 Group has a boat permanently moored there. Other waters with a fine Ferox pedigree include Loch Quoich, which has produced several large Ferox including the fifteen-year incumbency of the record (a fish of 8.87 kilograms –19lb 5oz), until that fateful day in Loch Awe in April 1993. Loch Garry in Inverness-shire also has a record-holding tradition including a fish of 19lb 2oz taken in 1965 by K. J. Grant on a Black Pennell fly. Simeon Cornwall (1860) recorded a fish of just two ounces under twenty pounds caught by trolling a small trout. A Ferox of 26lb was taken from Loch Garve in 1892, and a 27¼lb fish was taken in the outflow of Loch Assynt in 1870 by Dr H.H. Almond. These waters obviously have to form an important part of the choice of venues for the Ferox hunter in Scotland, but it is Loch Awe that has the past and present premier pedigree. It is there that we should most expect to see an advance on the current record.

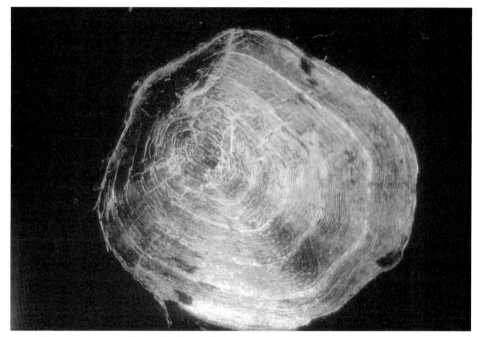

Scale from a 6-year-old 15lb ferox from Loch Awe (*A Stephen*)

The prediction has sound basis in fact. Three fish over 20lb have been found in recent years in or below the salmon ladder on the River Awe at its point of egress from the Pass of Brander; these comprise two of 23lb and one of 22lb. One of the 23lb fish was found as a partially-eaten carcass in the River Awe by the riparian Mr Jamie McGriggor of Ardchonell. The Ferox had no internal organs left and a substantial amount of flesh was missing from its body. Had it been whole and in good condition, for its length it would have probably weighed around 28lb. The other 23lb fish was a comparative youngster of six years, still in a rapid growth phase. Continued, reasonably good growth in this fish would have resulted in it soon attaining 30lb, especially as we know that Ferox in British waters can live for more than twenty years. Mr McGriggor later saw a much larger fish below the dam at Loch Awe. He estimated this fish, from his great experience as a salmon and trout angler, to be well in excess of 30lb. What were the chances that these fish were the biggest fish in the loch at the time? Not very high I would wager. One day the remarkable achievement of Mr Muir will be vindicated by being surpassed, and I want to be there when it happens, complete of course with camera and following the proper recording protocol.

No consideration of a new potential record trout should discount the famed ability of the great Irish loughs. The halcyon days of Lough Neagh may well be in the past, but there is no need, bearing in mind a recent recovery of the lough's ecosystem, to write it off entirely. Lough Neagh's huge expanse of water is shallow and biologically productive and therefore is very different in character from the classic Ferox lochs of the Highlands. The lough is famous for a type of trout locally termed 'Dollaghan'. This, according to my conversations with Professor Ferguson, is probably genetically distinct from other trout including Ferox, though it does attain weights in double figures of pounds. The giant trout of Lough Neagh may be a Ferox form known as the 'buddagh', a type thought similar to Scottish Ferox by writers such as T.T. Stoddart last century. Perhaps a record-busting buddagh still exists there feeding on the huge shoals of pollan for which the lough is also famous. Whether or not this is the case, there are many other Irish loughs that have the potential to produce fish well over twenty pounds. Lough Derg, for example, has produced fish up to 30½lb in weight, and Lough Ennell a Ferox of 26lb. Loughs Erne, Mask and Corrib also have great potential and are worth further effort.

Though Irish and Scottish waters appear to have more potential than their Welsh and English counterparts in producing large wild brown trout, it would not be surprising if Windermere or one of the other big Cumbrian lakes produced a 20lb Ferox. I hope for the sake of English trout fishing that this will be the case. Personally I regard the kind of thing that is going on at fisheries such as Dever Springs, as quite sad and no real alternative to wild trout fishing. I have often thought that claiming a record fish from such fisheries is roughly analogous to claiming a bison shot at Whipsnade.

Big or small, wild or domesticated, all trout start off life as an egg. Unfortunately very little is known about the spawning of Ferox. Being a member of the salmon family they frequently show the normal pattern of entering inflow streams in the autumn and depositing their eggs in redds made in suitable gravel. Being comparatively large fish, the requirements of Ferox are often met in the largest afferent streams. The homing behaviour of Ferox is probably at least as strong as any other salmonid fish in returning to the streams of their birth. In some Scandinavian lakes more than one group of Ferox may exist, each returning to their own native stream. What may come as a surprise to many anglers brought up on *Salar the Salmon* type life history stories reinforced by many high quality wildlife films depicting massive upstream migrations of fish overcoming all dangers and obstacles to reproduce, is that some populations of Ferox choose to spawn in the outflow streams of lakes. This means of course that the fry/parr have to be biologically 'programmed' in reverse mode when it comes to migrating to the mother lake. This apart, the choice of outflow spawning is not so strange as it may first appear. Outflow streams are by their very nature the largest running waters connected to a Ferox water. Whilst small inflowing streams may freeze solid during the winter or dry up completely in dry summers, much more stable conditions pertain to the outflow. This may offer considerable advantages in wild natural systems, but it is unfortunately the outflow that is most often radically altered when a lake is dammed to form a reservoir. Ferox spawning grounds may be seriously damaged in such situations. Even if a fish pass is built for the ingress of adult fish its design may not cater for the return of upward-migrating juvenile fish.

Outflow spawning is well documented in Scandinavia. The case remains open in the case of Scottish Ferox, but there is good circumstantial evidence that it occurs here also. Outflow spawning may be inferred from the 'famous' opening day that anglers have when they catch large trout below the barrage at Loch Rannoch where the infant River Tummel starts its journey to the sea near the village of Kinloch Rannoch. Frequently these fish are in very poor condition and appear to be kelts that have overwintered in the river after dropping out of Loch Rannoch to spawn. The autumn capture of huge Ferox in the fish trap in the River Awe as it exits the loch at the western end of the Pass of Brander is perhaps a further indication. Certainly Sir John Colqhoun of Luss mentions in his book *The Moor and the Loch* that the pass was not a good venue for Ferox fishing until the autumn, when the fish were making for the running water of this river to spawn. T.T. Stoddart also mentions this in his *Anglers Guide*: 'In the spawning season, when numbers of these fish (Ferox) push down to the outlet of the loch, they may be tempted to rise at the salmon lures ordinarily used on the River Awe'; presumably outlet spawning was common knowledge in the past, but has generally been forgotten in recent times.

Complete knowledge of Ferox maturation cycles remains elusive, but it appears that later maturation is a marked feature of their physiology compared to 'ordinary' trout. Annual spawning of individual fish does not always take place as it does in other forms of trout. It has often struck my colleagues and I, in both our angling and scientific samples of Ferox, that a wide range of states of sexual maturity exists in Ferox caught at various times of the year. One 17lb female Ferox caught at the end of September in Loch Arkaig comes particularly to mind. At this time of year

Examined in February this ferox was non-mature though 'adult' – no sign of previous spawning. (*A.F. Walker*)

one would expect to find obvious signs of full development of the egg mass indicative of imminent spawning in the later autumn period. This was simply not the case and it was clear that the fish was in excellent condition. This particular fish was simply not destined to spawn that year. Several other examples of both sexes indicating this have been encountered. It is also noticeable that early in the season, even on 'day one' the fifteenth of March, Ferox are captured in excellent condition, their reproductive organs showing no indication that spawning had taken place in the previous autumn/winter period. Conversely we have caught Ferox in mid-summer in very poor condition, their reproductive organs still showed signs of incomplete recovery from spawning. It is possible to capture both kinds of fish in the same sample. Spawning puts a heavy strain on the physiology of Ferox, and sufficient body mass may be diverted to the reproductive phase that it becomes difficult, even with an abundant supply of charr or other prey fish, for some Ferox totally to recover peak condition in the course of one season. This feature is to my mind the reason why some very thin, ugly Ferox are caught, giving rise to the negative images and pejorative comments associated with the fish. It is not merely a matter of ancient senescent fish in the declining years of their lives. The same fish caught eighteen months later might well be glass case specimens. Outflow fishing in the spring for Ferox should be avoided, perhaps even banned.

Further evidence of the strain of spawning on the growth and condition of Ferox comes from tagging experiments at Lake Tunhovdfjord, where marked fish caught as ascending adults showed no growth increment on their scales when recaptured in subsequent following seasons – a worrying fact to those basing their age determinations solely on scale readings. Otoliths, internal bony structures of the skull are more reliable but their use requires the death of the fish.

I am sure also that the various states of sexual maturation are in large part also responsible for the wide range of colour descriptions given in accounts of old. Adult but non-maturing fish are frequently more white-bellied and often have a silvery grey appearance not unlike a sea trout long resident in freshwater. Ripe or ripening fish tend to be more dark and bronzed. Kelt fish of course frequently exhibit all the dark ugliness of popular mythology. This should not however be confused with the genuine colour differences that exist in Ferox from individual waters. Loch Arkaig Ferox are very like dull sea trout, whereas Loch Rannoch fish seem cast from the best bronze. Loch Laggan in our experience produces the finest looking if not the largest Ferox in the country, with their golden bronze hues and striking spot patterns. Regardless of annual spawning or otherwise, the choice of inflow or outflow spawning sites or the colours in which they end up, the fate of Ferox fry in attaining the size that makes them an object of special interest to angler and scientist alike depends on the populations of charr that form a main part of their future food. It is now to the prey that we turn our attention.

2

The Prey: Arctic Charr, 'The Freshwater Reindeer'

One of the most evocative and abiding memories I have of my various trips to Scandinavia is of standing on the steps of a mountain cabin in the Jotunheimen mountains of Norway on a bright but cold August evening, looking out in wonder at a vast herd of reindeer. It was one of the first challenges to my previous prejudices I had about the environment of the Arctic, especially in terms of its biological richness and productivity. Like most Britons I had written off the Arctic as an unproductive desert, but the sight of such a prodigious number of these archetypal Arctic animals was the beginning of a process of reappraisal not only of the terrestrial environment of the mountains of Norway and Scotland, but also of the 'forgotten Arctic' of the larger freshwater bodies, home to another Arctic archetype, the charr.

Reindeer harness the limited potential of their environment by virtue of an interesting range of physiological and behavioural adaptations. Very well insulated of course against the extreme cold they also have a digestive system that is the home of bacteria that help the animal to digest poor quality vegetation. Seasonally they change their botanical menu and make wide-ranging migrations that maximise their intake of locally abundant food. They are expert at making the best of a bad situation. Their success in doing so enables other animals, including man, to fashion a lifestyle in this inhospitable world of high plateaux inthe far north.

My involvement in a number of research initiatives involving charr made me realise that the capacity for making a rich living amongst environmental poverty was a common feature of both animals, allowing them a wide circumpolar distribution. Just as numbers of racial variants of reindeer are found in a wide band around the northern hemisphere from the Canadian North-west Territories to Greenland, Scandinavia and northern Siberia, and also originally to the British Isles, charr mark their success in the Arctic by being the only member of the salmon family to have a totally circumpolar distribution.

In developing an extremely diverse range of local and regional forms and races as well as differentiated forms within the same lake, charr put the adaptability not only of reindeer, but many other Arctic animals to shame. This pot-pourri of physical, genetic and ecological variabilities presents scientists with a tangled matrix of diversity that makes untying the Gordian knot look like a job for the Cub Scouts. No system of analysis has so far fully resolved the issue of the independent status (or otherwise) of the various races or local and regional groupings. Even modern techniques of genetic fingerprinting threw up more new questions as answers were found to old ones. The variability seems ever more complex. Controversy still reigns among different scientific disciplines and a strategic resolution allowing a simple overview has not developed. The charr, of course, are oblivious to their success in their environment, their culinary qualities and their sheer physical beauty. Hopefully, and indeed thankfully, scientist and angler alike are not. Speaking as both, I know that among the people I have met in both spheres of life there is a passion for charr that is difficult to explain. It is a passion that in scientists creates an interest far beyond the call of normal professional objectivity; so much so in fact that an organisation has been formed by these scientists, known as the International Society of Arctic Charr Fanatics. The term 'fanatic' was chosen advisedly as this is how the challenge of charr affects the personality of even the most staid heads of fisheries departments, professors, 'philanderers' and other assorted 'ne'er-do-wells' who inhabit the halls of academe. Each country that is blessed with charr populations is allocated two members. I am proud to be one half of the Scottish membership, a distinction I share with Dr Peter Maitland of the Fish Conservation Centre near Stirling.

Scientific fanaticism for charr is in part a product of intellectual frustration. Charr are a conundrum for just about all the major issues of their ecology. Nothing in their biology appears clear-cut and concrete. Just when the rule book seems to be written at last, out comes another disclaimer to humble the over-confident. Even an apparently simple matter of their feeding preferences throws up confusing inconsistencies. The classic studies of Dr Winnifred Frost of the Windermere Laboratory on the charr of the English Lake District have greatly influenced the general view of the feeding ecology of charr in the British Isles. The prevailing perception of charr occurring together with brown trout, and other species such as perch and pike, is that they are mainly planktivorous, feeding on items such as daphnia (water fleas). Other food items such as aquatic insect larvae or fish would be considered of minor importance. This view has long been held in the main because little information on the ecology of charr in the other countries of the UK has been available, and until recently such data as has been available has been confirmatory. In the last decade or so new information from the Scottish Highlands has, however, started to change the picture somewhat. Studies in a number of lochs in the Grampian Highlands have revealed the much greater importance of bottom-living

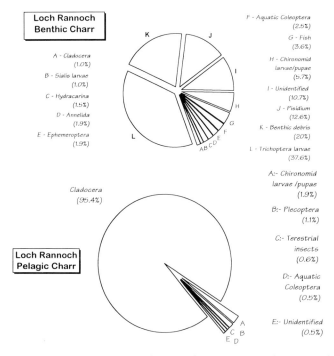

Loch Rannoch
Benthic Charr

A - Cladocera
(1.0%)
B - Sialis larvae
(1.0%)
C - Hydracarina
(1.5%)
D - Annelida
(1.9%)
E - Ephemeroptera
(1.9%)

F - Aquatic Coleoptera
(2.5%)
G - Fish
(3.6%)
H - Chironomid
larvae/pupae
(5.7%)
I - Unidentified
(10.7%)
J - Pisidium
(12.6%)
K - Benthic debris
(20%)
L - Trichoptera larvae
(37.6%)

Loch Rannoch
Pelagic Charr

Cladocera
(95.4%)

A:- Chironomid
larvae /pupae
(1.9%)
B:- Plecoptera
(1.1%)
C:- Terestrial
insects
(0.6%)
D:- Aquatic
Coleoptera
(0.5%)
E:- Unidentified
(0.5%)

Stomach contents of two forms of Charr in Loch Rannoch

From Walker et al 1988

food organisms in the diet of charr especially in the spring and early summer. In Loch Rannoch, one of the two forms of charr known to occur here is a specialist bottom feeder the whole year round, occasionally augmenting its diet with fish.

The importance of bottom-living food items in the diet of Grampian charr and the seasonal variation have strong echoes of the much more detailed investigations of the diet of charr in Swedish and Norwegian lakes. This is interesting because in many ways the overall biological and environmental characteristics of the Grampian Highlands place them with greater affinity to western Scandinavian mountain ranges than to other upland areas of the UK. However, the spring and early summer importance of bottom food has also been observed in Loch Maree in the western Highlands and in Loch Doon in Galloway. It may be inadvisable to extrapolate the results of research in one part of the UK wholesale to another, and it may very well be the case that comparative work in western Scandinavia has more relevance to the Highland situation. More widespread research should be considered as a prophylactic for the prevention of 'little charrlander complex'! Another major difference I have noted in diet of Scottish charr compared to Windermere charr is the absence of charr eggs in the Scottish charr I have examined. Having said that and charr being the kind of animals they are, I

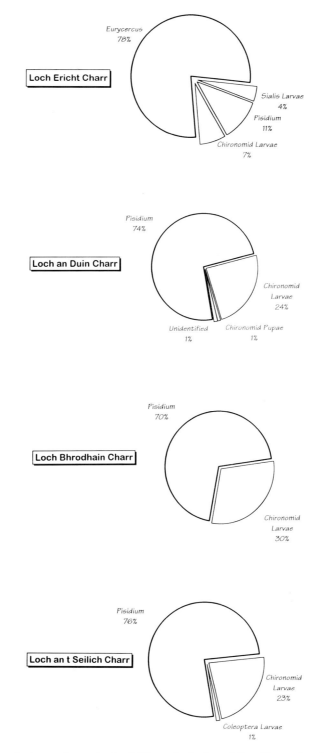

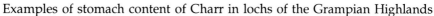
Examples of stomach content of Charr in lochs of the Grampian Highlands

shall probably have humbly to retract this statement in the very near future. However, I feel more confident that no researcher in Britain will ever have to describe seagull droppings as a major food item of charr, as is the case in Lake Laguna on Jan Mayen (perhaps flexibility of food choice in charr is an understatement!) Another interesting example of this is shown by the ready manner in which charr in Highland lochs quickly took up the option of living under the now all-too-common rearing facilities for salmon smolts and rainbow trout present in many of our larger waters. Here the charr willingly accessed the precipitation of waste food and indeed any escaped juvenile fish. One of the most obvious results was increased growth leading among other things to a rapid increase in the rod-caught record for charr. Anglers may be happy at this, but the long-term ecological implications could be much less rosy.

Charr have a capacity to inhabit a greater range of depths than trout, and just as reindeer make migrations to access locally abundant food sources so their freshwater counterpart can access food in the deep water zone, the mid-water zone and surface area of a lake within a very short space of time. In Lake Blasjön in Sweden scientists have found surface food items in a dwarf race of charr captured at over 300 feet down. Trout on the other hand, seem to be much more rigid in behaviour, generally preferring to access snails, shrimps and aquatic insect larvae in the shallow water shore zone. Some of course as we know switch to a fish diet and become Ferox. The overall interaction of charr and trout in the habitat they share, apart from just the Ferox/charr relationship, has long interested scientists and anglers. It has been a major research interest in the Scandinavian countries, especially in regard to the effects of harnessing natural lakes as sources of hydro-electric power production. The general concept developed is of a distinct food and habitat segregation between the two species; however, this is not written on tablets of stone. While it is a useful starting point to consider the trout as being a shallow water predator on the bigger food items such as caddis larvae and freshwater shrimps, and charr as consumers of deep and open water resources of pea mussels and plankton, it is important not to apply this too rigidly. Loch Rannoch is a case in point, for in some ways the diet of the bottom-living charr here shows some features in common with trout, in particular in its consumption of caddis larvae and the freshwater shrimp *Gammarus*. The food of the mid-water form of charr found in Rannoch does however conform to the overall biological rule of thumb.

When either species occupies a lake without the presence of the other their diets are remarkably similar, with the shallow water food items being the preferred choice of both charr and trout. Normally, in the case of cohabitation, the charr does not compete well with trout for this preferred resource and has to use its flexibility in making the best of a poorer option.

Food of Charr and Trout in Loch Ness

	Charr		Brown Trout	
	Total Points	%	Total Points	%
Daphnia	172.9	26.55	36.0	15.46
Bythotrephes	235.8	36.20	34.2	14.69
Leptodora	75.4	11.58	6.3	2.71
Bosmina	14.1	2.16	—	—
Corepods	13.0	2.0	—	—
Chironomids	77.4	11.88	3.7	1.59
Fish	—	—	93.0	39.95
Pisidium SP.	6.1	0.94	—	—
Other Benthos	37.0	5.68	—	—
Aquatic insects	—	—	3.0	1.30
Aerial insects	19.6	3.01	56.6	24.31
Total	651.3	100.31	232.8	100.01

	Charr		Brown Trout	
	Total Points	%	Total Points	%
Daphnia	28	25.93	3	6.52
Bythotrephes	27	25.0	2	4.35
Leptodora	1	0.93	—	—
Bosmina	—	—	—	—
Corepods	1	0.93	—	—
Chironomids	5	4.63	—	—
Fish	—	—	19	41.30
Pisidium SP.	—	—	—	—
Other Benthos	6	5.56	—	—
Aquatic insects	—	—	1	2.17
Aerial insects	—	—	7	15.22

(Martin & Shine 1994)

However, the tables are turned in very severe Arctic conditions and there are recorded cases, as at Lake Breivatn in the high mountains of southern Norway, of charr almost wiping out trout populations under marginal conditions. Charr also score the 'Brownie points' under the changed conditions after a natural lake has been converted to a hydro-electric reservoir. In such conditions the main feeding areas for the trout in the shore zone are radically altered by water level fluctuations. Swedish research has suggested up to a seventy per cent loss of production of food items normally accessed by trout. The open and deep water zones are much less affected and consequently the charr are relatively much better off than the trout which do not compete well with charr in these areas. Indeed, charr generally do that much better under these reservoir conditions, that such waters should be considered as charr lakes with trout present rather than the normal British perception of considering the reverse to be true.

This otherwise comparatively simple dietary picture is complicated by other competitive interactions when more than one form of charr is present or other species of fish, such as powan or vendace, occur. Generally charr are at a competitive disadvantage to powan, vendace and other types of whitefish. Introductions of whitefish to lakes previously only containing charr and trout have caused the collapse or severe reduction of the charr population. In this situation the only role left for the charr is as a deep water bottom feeder, becoming the charr equivalent of Ferox. According to my Swedish colleague Dr Johan Hammar of the Freshwater Institute at Drottningholm, this latter phenomenon is facilitated by the presence of the smelt *Osmerus eperlanus*. Charr and indeed other plankton feeding fish species have also been detrimentally affected by introductions of invertebrate animals, strangely enough introduced to provide food for fish. The classic example of this is with the opossum shrimp, *Mysis relicta*, which was widely introduced in Scandinavian reservoirs during the 1960s and 1970s in an attempt to redress the loss of food items after lakes were converted to hydro-electric reservoirs. This shrimp is very tolerant of the conditions found in reservoirs, and as an individual food item makes an excellent meal for charr or trout. Unfortunately the shrimps' own varied diet includes young plankton animals which are important food for juvenile fish. Though early promise was shown in the improved quality of adult fish feeding on *Mysis*, eventually there was a disastrous collapse of some important commercial fisheries for charr. Who would have predicted fish being out-competed by their own food? This was more than just embarrassing, for serious litigation was entered into. This was great news for the legal profession, but not of good cheer to the scientific community.

From the above the reader will have seen it is impossible to describe the major features of the biology of charr without mentioning physical variation between and within populations occurring in different lakes and in the same water body. Even more than with Ferox and other forms of trout, encompassing this variation in a classification system that does justice to the reality of the variation itself and the intellectual agony of the scientists who have struggled and indeed still are struggling to produce it, is a monumental task. It is so bad in fact that it is known in the world of charr research as The Charr Problem. Having said that we would all admit deep down it is also very inspiring and a major motivation for charr fanaticism. I am going to tell you right now that a solution to the above problem will not be found in the pages of this book. Only an indication of its intriguing nature can be given for even whole volumes of literature on charr, including major books, have not fully covered it. New research constantly requires modification to be made to prevailing theories. The task is not hopeless or thankless, just very demanding on adrenal glands and brain cells.

The wide variety of physical appearance in charr from one location to another in the British Isles was long recognised by very much the same group of early writers on trout mentioned in the first chapter. Tate Regan, for example, classified British charr as belonging to fifteen distinct species. In their summaries of the various descriptions given to charr there was a penchant for assigning personal appellations to particularly distinct local forms. Thus we have such examples as Willoughby's Charr in Windermere, Coles' Charr in Ireland and Malloch's Charr from Scotland. Such a personalisation is no longer in vogue, although as a co-discoverer of a new form of charr myself it would have been very flattering indeed to have it named after me. However, charr are humblers of the 'unco guid' as Rabbie Burns would say, so the Swede Carl von Linne (Linnaeus) probably saved all charr scientists from bruised egos when he established the internationally recognised Latinised binomial classification system.

The site-to-site variation in the physical appearance of charr does grip the imagination in a very profound way, but this pales to insignificance compared to the scientific passion which is aroused when more than one race, form or species of charr occurs in the same lake. The causative agency for the derivation of these multiple forms is at the very hub of the evolutionary concept. Arguments basically centre around the various forms evolving from a single common ancestor which invaded any given lake at the cessation of the glacial period, versus the theory of multiple invasions of stocks which were already different through being isolated from each other for a much longer period during major ice ages. This latter theory has more credence for me, but we must never underestimate the adaptive capacity of charr in new situations. The problem of assembling the various pieces into even a crude jigsaw picture is made much more difficult by the fact that the various forms of charr can either maintain their genetic integrity or cross-breed with the other forms, producing intermediate types of fish. Much depends on the local circumstances allowing maintenance of separate spawning sites and/or times. Deliberate or accidental introductions by man of charr from other lakes may break down the barriers previously maintaining discrete stocks. This is a major concern to be faced with more and more fish farmers turning their attentions to the aquaculture of charr in Highland lochs. In what I consider to be one of the most gross acts of ecological stupidity in the history of the Highlands since the introduction of Cheviot and Blackface sheep, some fish farmers have not only begun the inter-watershed transfer of Scottish charr stocks but have also started to import foreign strains of charr. This, to my mind, makes selling tartan made in Hong Kong as a genuine Scottish product look like an act of extreme cultural and economic wisdom. Perhaps an even better analogy would be removing for ever the potential of Highland distilleries to make pure malt whisky by irreversibly mixing it with Vietnamese vodka. This is how reckless some fish farmers have already been. The Highlands are richly blessed with charr populations. The introduction of foreign stocks is not only biologically inadvisable, it is plainly completely unnecessary and a waste of time, effort and money.

The foul hand of human greed and stupidity notwithstanding, we still have a rich legacy of diverse charr forms occupying a wide range of often very challenging habitats throughout their northern circumpolar distribution. Like their relatives, trout and salmon, charr are capable of living in salt water and have migratory forms with a life history very similar to sea trout. The clear-cut physical and metabolic changes which occur in young salmon when transforming from the parr to the smolt stage are not so clearly marked in charr. The freshwater residence phase is much more variable and extended than in either sea trout or salmon, and today sea-going charr are

Deep water form of charr from Loch Ericht similar in appearance to Loch Rannoch Benthic form.

only common north of a latitude of 65°. At present no migratory charr are known in Britain, but I have heard unconfirmed reports of charr running the River Hope and River Naver in northern Scotland. Such locations are the most likely ones if migratory charr were still extant in the British Isles. The fact that we are not certain of such a basic point is a sad indictment of our state of knowledge of the fish in this country. However, this is no surprise to me as a new form of charr was found in Loch Rannoch as recently as 1975. Like all the best scientific discoveries this happened by accident. This was also the case in 1989 in Loch Tummel when an Irishman making a mistake in setting a net meant for perch caught a number of charr, similar in appearance to the deep water charr of Rannoch. Both events occurred just a few miles from the Freshwater Laboratory, Pitlochry, so there are no grounds for scientific complacency. There are probably many more such discoveries to be made. I hope to be involved in some of them.

Regardless of whether or not migratory charr occur in Britain today we can be certain that all of our present, permanently freshwater resident charr populations were derived from a migratory stock or, perhaps more likely, several stocks of charr entering the newly deglaciated river systems some 12,000 to 13,000 years ago. There is growing evidence that at least two genetically distinct groups of charr were involved in the re-colonisation process. Scandinavian scientists, such as my colleagues in ISACF Dr Johan Hammar and Professor Lennart Nyman, similarly think this to be case in their region. Indeed, they consider it likely that three distinct groups re-invaded as the glaciers waned. These three forms exist as a bottom- and fish-feeding form which spawns in running water, a plankton-feeding form which spawns in still water, and a more ecologically flexible form which is also a lake rather than a river spawner. There are many lakes in Scandinavia that have at least two of these forms, and the occurrence of multiple forms of charr in one lake is considered relatively commonplace. Their study elucidates many of the principles of evolutionary biology and is one of the most exciting aspects of charr research.

For many years the only known example of the occurrence of more than one form of charr in any British water was Windermere. Once again we have to thank Dr Winnifred Frost for a classic scientific discourse on the phenomenon. Her seminal work was then followed up by Dr Chris Mills and Dr John Partington who reviewed the position of the Windermere forms with reference to eight other English and Welsh charr lakes, and also to Loch Doon in Galloway, southern Scotland. The existence of the two discrete Windermere populations based on physical features and the choice of autumn or spring spawning behaviour was further confirmed by genetic analysis. In a number of biological characteristics the charr of Ennerdale were discovered to be distinctly different from the other Cumbrian populations. The Welsh charr and those of Loch Doon were not only markedly different from each other but also from the Cumbrian charr populations. Interestingly, Dr Sheila Hartley of Stirling University, who is now using a wider range of genetic analyses in her studies on charr, found that Loch Doon fish were more like charr from the Scottish Highlands than those in the Lake District. Considering the close geographical proximity of Cumbria and Galloway this is somewhat surprising, as a reasonable assumption might have been to consider a common origin from an original stock of migratory charr from the Irish Sea. To my mind all this points to a complicated picture of post-glacial invasions of charr from different sea basins, not only from large glacial refuges on the international scale, but also on a more local British scale.

Just about at the same time as Dr Mills and his colleagues published on the above, my colleague Andrew Walker and I published, in conjunction with Dr Andrew Gardner, the first of two papers on the discovery of two discrete types of charr in Loch Rannoch in Highland Perthshire. These works, apart from doubling at a stroke the known occurrence of this phenomenon in the British Isles, added more fuel to the debate on the mechanisms for the evolution of such variations. In some ways, especially in their physical appearance and feeding ecology, these two different forms were even more dissimilar to each other than is the case in Windermere. There was a difference in spawning site selection between the two forms as there is in Windermere. One form, which feeds mainly on bottom-living food and lives in deep water much of the time, chooses to spawn in the inflowing River Gaur at the western end of the loch. Spawning time for this form, termed the benthic form in scientific parlance, is usually at the end of October. In consequence I facetiously call this the 'Halloween charr'. The other form, termed the pelagic charr, feeds on plankton and spawns around mid-October on the shore line of the loch. Since the discovery was first described, more recent work by Dr Colin Adams of Glasgow University suggests that the benthic form may consist of two discrete populations in itself, although the difference in this case is not so great as between the two main forms. We may be seeing here more than one mechanism operating to allow the development of variant types: an invasion of two already genetically distinct ancestors of the modern pelagic and benthic forms at the termination of the glacial period, followed by subsequent differentiation of the benthic form by selection of more than one spawning site.

Work at Rannoch is at an early stage compared to Windermere and, unlike its Cumbrian counterpart, the loch is not in the happy position of having a major research institute on its shores. With the possibility of Loch Rannoch having at least three distinct forms of brown trout – including our beloved Ferox – as well as three forms of charr, it certainly deserves one. There is now growing evidence that other large Highland lochs contain more than one form of charr; indeed it would not be surprising if it were a common occurrence. Loch Ericht, for example, contains a form of charr that has very close similarities to the benthic charr of Rannoch, in addition to at least one other form. The truth is we have not looked hard enough at or done justice to our sub-Arctic inheritance. Even our largest, most famous lochs have not been fully investigated. Here we are, in the best-mapped country in the world, with a long history of university education, and we still do not know what kind of fish we have in our major inland waters. Come to think of, it we cannot even prove or disprove the existence of a dinosaur in Loch Ness! Time for a good dram and some serious introspection.

Apart from invasions from distant and nearby glacial refuges, purely on a spatial basis we have to think of invasions widely separated in time. The main history of recent glaciation in the British Isles shows wide fluctuation in the severity and extent of glacier formation. There were comparatively warmer periods between the main, extremely cold epochs which may have allowed repeated access to sea charr at the margins of the ice cap. Charr can survive many years in lakes that are only ice-free for a few weeks a year, a classic example being Lake Hazen on Ellesmere Island in the Canadian Northern Territories. Conceivably stocks could have survived in isolation for some time until a new migration of, by this time, genetically different charr arrived.

Of greater significance in this respect are the final phases of the deglaciation process. We know that the main phase of deglaciation that took place 12,000 to 13,000 years ago was followed by a warm period, where temperatures were fairly similar to, if not slightly warmer than, today's. This warmer period lasted at least a thousand years, perhaps longer. The chances are that this would have meant that migratory charr were no longer present and that the various resident populations were isolated from each other as well as from the exchange of genetic material from sea-run fish. Thus a differentiation of local stocks could begin or be, more likely, enhanced.

This comparatively short warm spell was then followed by a further cold period that initiated a new development of glacier formation. This secondary period of glacier development is known in geological circles as the Loch Lomond Re-advance. It was a comparatively minor and short-lived glacial advance with the main glaciation centred round the south-west Highlands. Much of lowland Britain and the eastern Highlands escaped glaciation completely, although they once more experienced a climate sufficiently Arctic in nature to allow the return of migratory charr. This would certainly have created a further opportunity for a new form of genetically different charr to enter the domain of those aboriginal populations established millennia before. The only other time a fresh wave of 'sea invaders' could have conceivably occurred is during the 'Little Ice Age' of the late Middle

Ages. However, this is much less likely and we might have expected some form of mention of sea charr in historical records.

Long-term isolation in sea basin refuges that escaped glaciation is no doubt the main mechanism for allowing differentiation of charr stocks from a common ancestor to occur. That begs the question of where these refuges lay. Glaciation swamped the land mass of western Europe with a sea of ice up to 3,000 feet thick. Most of Scandinavia and the greater part of Ireland and Britain, as far south as the Thames simply disappeared for thousands of years. Charr may have run the rivers from the open sea to the south-west of England and Ireland. Land conditions here were probably not unlike southern Greenland today. With so much water tied up in the form of ice, land to the west of Ireland and the Hebrides almost certainly would have had rivers harbouring sea charr. There is some evidence from the genetic analysis of trees in the north-west Highlands that they are distinct from trees on the eastern side of the country. The suggestion here is that during the height of the glaciation a refuge, to the west of present-day Lewis and Harris, existed on land now inundated by a rise in sea level when the ice melted. From here the trees could re-invade the watershed to the west of the mountain spine (Drumalbyn) which still separates them from their arboreal cousins, who 'rode out the storm' on the dry land of southern Europe and recolonised from the south-east. If this is the case with trees then why not for adaptable fish like charr. The geographical distances

Charr from Lake Torrön, Sweden. (*J Hammar*)

involved in this hypothesis are tiny compared to the evidence cited by my fellow charr fanatic, Anders Klemetsen of the University of Tromsø, in his overview of the derivation of genetically distinct forms of charr in Norway. Anders, in his 1990 presentation to the 6th workshop of The International Society of Arctic Charr Fanatics in Murmansk, put forward a compelling case for the concurrent invasion of at least two groups of charr into Norway, one from a glacial refuge to the south of the British Isles and another from the Laptev Sea to the north of central Siberia. There is also some evidence from recent genetic studies that Siberian-origin charr may also have emigrated to British waters. The case of the pollan in Ireland is collateral evidence for this possibility as the pollan is genetically closer to the whitefish of Siberia than it is to its nearest British relatives. Intriguing stuff all this, and perhaps the reader will now be getting an insight into what really 'burns the scientist up'.

Getting round to the subject of Siberian charr was no coincidence, for there is a certain lake in the Chukotka region which demonstrates very clearly what happens when the evolution of separate forms of charr is not interrupted by the advance and retreat of glaciers. It also provides a further classic example of the adaptability of charr under extremely harsh conditions. In addition it also indicates the sheer and utter guts that makes charr fanatics a special breed of scientists. Our rejected 'recruits' are sent to be trained as officers in the SAS or since we are here dealing with our Russian contingent, the forces of the Speznatz. Life here is easier than it is in ISACF and you have more chance of the general public appreciating your achievements.

The lake in question is called Lake El'Gygytgyn. This is a word used by the native Chukchi people and I have noticed that even my fellow fanatics in Russia have difficulty with the phonetics until they have had at least three large vodkas, or a major digestive upset. Three large malt whiskies are a suitable substitute. It simply means the 'white lake', but that is all that is simple about it. Investigations by Russian geologists indicate the lake was formed 3.5 million years ago by the impact of a large meteor. This impact left a hole twelve kilometres (7.5 miles) in diameter, some 179 metres (587 feet) deep. The average depth of the lake is 100 metres (328 feet). The cold dry, continental climate, while allowing Arctic conditions to prevail, provided insufficient precipitation to allow major glacial advances. Thus for most of its history the charr population have avoided the extinction that befell their western European and Scandinavian cousins. The evolution of incipient variant forms of charr could therefore progress in a way that was prevented in heavily glaciated regions and gives an insight into what may happen in places like Rannoch or Windermere given sufficient time.

Known only to European Russians since 1930, and then only by aerial survey, the fish populations of the lake were brought, in the summer of

1978, to the attention of fellow charr fanatic Dr Mikhail Skopets of the then Soviet Institute of Biological Problems of the North, at Magadan. Chukchi reindeer herders informed him that this remote lake contained charr unlike any they had seen in other lakes.

His fanaticism flamed to a frenzy, Mikhail managed to persuade the authorities to fund an expedition the following year. Braving July and August snowstorms and summer sub-zero temperatures, the expedition discovered that the lake contained Arctic grayling, a species of bullhead and a species of large (up to 12lb in weight) fish-eating charr known as the Boganid charr. This form of charr has a very limited known distribution

The boganid charr of Siberia, whose dietary habits led to the discovery of a new species and new genus of charrl. (*Fred Kircheis*)

area, being only recorded in a few other lakes in the Taimyr region. Its stomach contents however were as interesting as the fish itself, for they included the remains of a form of charr new to science and found only in Lake El'Gygytgyn. Actual samples of the new charr, named the Small-mouth charr *Salvelinus elgyticus,* were only obtained by the perseverance of Mikhail in remaining behind alone, in very severe weather conditions, while the rest of the expedition returned to base. He obtained a sample of 200 spawning charr in September, thus bringing these fish well into the corpus of science. Later investigation proved this charr to be a plankton-feeding species which lived at depths of up to 100 metres.

However, the culinary intrigues of the big Boganid charr did not cease at this juncture. Back at base, several months later, investigation of the skeletal remains of Boganid charr stomach contents revealed not only the remains of

The two new discoveries of Mikhail Spopets.
Top: Thew new genus of longfin charr
Bottom: The new species of smallmouth charr. (*Fred Kircheis*)

the recently discovered Smallmouth charr, but also another type unknown to science. It was to be a further six years before Mikhail Skopets could raise enough funds to return in 1985 for further sampling. There is only a two-month ice-free season in this lake, making sampling a very difficult operation indeed. Frustratingly to begin with, attempts to find the new charr failed, with the only further evidence being found in Boganid stomachs. Acting on a hunch, Mikhail set his nets to a depth of 200 feet and succeeded not only in hauling up a new species, but a new genus! Called the Long-fin charr, because of the exaggerated development of its fins, particularly the pectoral fins, this fish was placed in the scientific binomial nomenclature as *Salvethymus svetovidovi*. Salvethymus was chosen for the generic label because the fish reminded the discoverers of both charr and grayling, although the fish is in no way whatsoever a hybrid. The large fins are apparently used to assist the fish in making very precise short movements in capturing the deep water plankton animals that are its main food. We really owe this discovery to the flexible feeding behaviour of the Boganid charr. Feeding on the Long-fin charr in depths where the temperature seldom exceeds thirty-six Fahrenheit it ascends to digest its prey in the warmer waters near inflow streams, where the temperature is some ten degrees higher. The Long-fin charr is thought to spend the bulk of its life at

The name longfin charr is a good one as can be seen in this photograph of an amazing new discovery by charr fanatic Mikhail Skopets. (*Fred Kircheis*)

depths greater than 200 feet, spawning in May or June up to 300 feet below the ice. Intriguing as all this suffering for science is, I am more than happy to be at Rannoch at Halloween, even if we are still some three million years away from the complete separation of the charr stocks as at El'Gygytgyn.

The vast Arctic and sub-Arctic territories of the former Soviet Union also contain a fascinating variety of other Arctic charr forms in addition to the discrete species and genus of the above ancient crater lake. In western Siberia and in European Russia these forms are generally considered to be contained in the envelope of what is known as the *Salvelinus alpinus* 'complex'. Difficult as this is to decipher and describe, the situation in the water systems draining to the Pacific 'Far East' is even more complex. This extra complexity is shared by workers in western Canada and Alaska as part of a shared evolutionary history that also provides interesting parallels in forest species composition, general ecology and human cultures. The well-known linking action of the Bering sea basin provided more than just opportunities for human colonisation of North America. In terms of interest to charr fanatics such as myself the connection is most direct and apparent in the mutual occurrence of a charr commonly known as the 'Dolly Varden' (*Salvelinus malma*). This charr not only occurs on both the Russian and American sides of the Pacific, it also migrates between river systems in both areas, involving sea and river journeys of over a thousand kilometres.

The relationship of the Dolly Varden to the Arctic Charr has been the subject of much scientific soul-searching, and the old debate of the 'lumpers and splitters' was, if anything, even more intense than it was over their European cousins. In both the North American and the Asian side of the Pacific the debate did not just have to take into account jointly occurring (sympatric) permanent freshwater resident charr of different genetic background, but also sea-going forms. In coming to conclusions about the relative positions of the various charrs in the family tree, both Russian and North American workers had to work over vast distances and huge watersheds. The logistical problems in Britain pale to insignificance beside this. We are very lucky indeed to have such nearby natural 'laboratories' like Rannoch and Windermere.

At the 6th ISACF workshop in 1990 at Murmansk, I listened with a great deal of interest and admiration to a seminar presented my Russian colleague Dr Igor Chershnev on his work on the charrs of the Chukchi, Bering and Okhotsk sea basins. This mainly centred round resolving the genetic and ecological relationships between *Salvelinus malma*, *Salvelinus leucomaenis*, *Salvelinus levanidovi* and *Salvelinus taranetzi*. Igor concluded that the Dolly Varden (*S. malma*) was indeed a distinct species from the others sharing a Pacific origin with *Salvelinus leucomaenis*, whilst *Salvelinus taranetzi* was a member of the Arctic group. The position of 'Levandov's charr' however remained unresolved due to the occurrence of characteristics of both Arctic and Pacific forms. At much the same time on the Alaskan side of the Pacific fellow charr fanatic Fred de Cicco was carrying out his own research into the Dolly Varden charr. Two forms of Dolly Varden are known to occur in North America: a northern form, which ranges from the Alaskan Peninsula to Canada's Mackenzie river; and a southern form which occurs from south-eastern Alaska to as far south as California. Just as in Arctic charr, both sea-going and freshwater resident forms occur. Fred worked mainly on the northern migratory form which is of recreational and subsistence value to Alaskan rural communities. His efforts concentrated on the Noatak, Wulik and Kivalina rivers.

His studies on the life history of these populations revealed that two groups of spawners existed: a summer spawning group which spawned in late August/mid-September; and an autumn spawning group spawning from mid-September/early October. Stocks homed to their nursery grounds but mixed with other stocks in non-spawning areas. Migration movements were studied by using traditional and radio transmitter tags. This revealed that the charr had complex migration patterns involving more than just limited coastal journeys in the sea. The most dramatic finding was that two of the tagged fish had travelled from the Wulik river in Alaska to the Anadyr river of the then Soviet Far East. The distance involved was an incredible 1,700 kilometres.

As well as the Dolly Varden, Arctic charr share the boreal regions of Canada and America with two other of its cousins from whom it is clearly distinct. These are the North American lake trout (*Salvelinus namaycush*, sometimes given the generic *Cristivomer*) and the brook trout (*Salvelinus fontinalis)* of eastern Canada and the USA. It is indeed unfortunate that these two charr are called trout in common parlance. That they are certainly not, but in some ways they occupy ecological roles similar to trout in Europe. Brook trout have been introduced to Britain and Scandinavia, but generally do not compete well with the native brown trout. This latter has impacted negatively on brook trout when introduced to North America. When brook trout and Arctic charr occur together in their home ranges they frequently display a similar habitat and food segregation as noted in the charr and brown trout in Europe. At the limits of their respective ranges they may naturally hybridise, as in the Fraser river in eastern Canada. Sadly this has been a point of origin of charr import to the Scottish Highlands for aquaculture. Such natural mixing is the very hammer striking on the anvil of evolution, but it is a dangerous tool in the hands of thoughtless mankind. All the species of the genus Salvelinus can be easily hybridised artificially and can produce very interesting, beautiful and sometimes apparently useful offspring. In North America, lake trout and brook trout have been hybridised to produce 'splake', a popular sporting quarry, and in Europe brook trout and charr have been crossed, for among other reasons, experiments to produce fish tolerant of waters affected by acid rain. Lake trout have been introduced, with no great general success, to Scandinavian lakes and have been artificially crossed with native charr. Was the experiment worth the mess? This is an open question and hopefully one that will not be answered on the back of the destruction of the genetic integrity of British charr. Natural hybrids between lake trout and Arctic charr have been described in North America. My colleague Johan Hammar described such a case from Labrador.

Unlike brook trout, the North American lake trout has not been successfully introduced to British waters. Many aspects of its ecology parallel that of Ferox very closely and its introduction may have negative impacts. Luckily the legislation prohibiting import of foreign fish species is now in place and hopefuly we will be spared the threat posed by fish farmers to our Arctic charr stocks. That charr themselves can occupy a Ferox role has already been commented on elswhere, but it is one that has evolved with the presence of brown trout over millennia. This would not be the case with the lake trout of the New World.

The extreme conditions of the far north, such as those at the Siberian lake El'Gygytgyn, no doubt help explain the slow growth and great longevity of the charr. The largest Long-fin charr captured there was thirty-three centimetres (thirteen inches) long and was thirty years old. The main component in the sample comprised fish of between twenty to thirty centimetres which were generally in the age range eighteen to twenty-three years. Boganid charr reach ages of up to twenty years, and the Smallmouth charr twenty-six years. Slow growth and the great age of charr in unexploited Arctic lakes is a common feature not only in Siberia,

Average Length(cm) at Age of Charr in 5 Scottish Lochs

Age Group	Laggan	Garry	Awe	Ness	Rannoch, (pelagic)[1]
1	?	12.3	?	?	?
2	15.1	15.8	15.6	15.1	15.1
3	18.1	18.5	18.2	16.8	20.8
4	19.6	20.3	20.0	21.5	22.8
5	20.5	19.9	20.0	24.1	22.7
6	21.2	?	?	?	24.7
7	?	?	?	?	26.0

[1]based on Walker et al. 1988

but also in Canada, Alaska and Greenland. In exploited lakes the older age classes disappear and a younger age structure develops. The age and growth parameters in British charr are not well-known, though the work at Windermere is a shining exception. Here charr have been harvested for centuries so one would not expect the longevity experienced in the virgin lakes of the north. What is surprising is that the charr populations of unexploited Highland lochs seem to consist of comparatively young small fish. The oldest Scottish charr I have examined was eleven years old, a comparatively large benthic fish from Rannoch. Very few records of charr older than ten years have been recorded from Highland lochs. In many of the lochs familiar to me most of the adult charr sampled seem to consist of four to six-year-old fish. The standard method of determining ages from scale readings does not work very well with charr. The scales are about half the size of an equivalent sized trout and frequently the alternate zonation of narrow winter bands of rings with broader summer ones is difficult to discern; instead, otoliths are used, similar in shape to weathered Stone Age

[1]Loch Laggan Charr(sample of 228)

Age Group	% in Sample	Mean Length(cm)	Mean Weight(g)
2	2.2	15.1	60.0
3	16.2	18.1	80.9
4	50.4	19.6	100.5
5	22.4	20.5	107.9
6	8.8	21.2	122.5

[1]based on Greer and Collen 1982

arrowheads. Charr otoliths are just a few millimetres long and they may continue to grow and develop annual rings even if the fish does not grow in length. Thus back-calculation of growth is not the viable option it often is with trout.

A charr of about 300 to 450 grams (twelve to sixteen ounces) would for many years have been considered a large fish in most British waters. However, since the advent of salmon smolt-rearing facilities in Highland lochs the propensity of charr to take advantage of waste food passing through the cages has resulted in an astounding increase in the rod-caught record for charr. In 1984 the record was just over 800 grams (about 1.75lb), from Loch Insh in Strathspey. Frequent breaking of the record resulted in a string of fish in excess of 3,000 grams from Loch Arkaig, with the record occasionally lasting less than month. Anglers have proved very adaptable in learning to fish near the cages and I have heard reports of fish of over 8lb (3,625 grams) being captured. I believe it is only a matter of time before a charr of over 10lb is taken. Though this proves the inherent growth potential of native charr and makes the import of foreign strains look even more unnecessary; to my mind it also detracts from the spirit of sportsmanship. However, these are still wild fish making a choice, which is more than can be said about the deliberate rearing of record trout as a commercial enterprise. Such large charr are in no way near the potential limit for the species. Sea charr can reach weights of 30lb, and the fish-eating charr of southern Scandinavian lakes can exceed 20lb. It is not beyond the bounds of possibility that such huge charr also live in the depths of Loch Rannoch or Loch Ness. These 'giant' charr show many of the characteristics of Ferox, including their intimate reliance on the structure and availability of prey species. Studies by my colleague and fellow charr fanatic Dr Johan Hammar on Swedish lakes indicate that Ferox charr develop in situations where the normal charr role is taken up or limited by competing species of whitefish. Further to this, the occurrence of smelt is extremely important in allowing the charr to access an intermediate sized food item on the way to attaining a size where they can then prey on the adult whitefish.

During the above descriptions of various other aspects of the biology of charr, more than passing reference has been made to their spawning behaviour. This is intrinsically interesting apart from its importance in marking, or indeed causing, the distinctive divisions of race or species. As you may be expecting by now, this aspect of their lifestyle is highly diverse in nature and confusingly does not always conform to the 'standard package' of salmonid spawning characteristics. Having said that, it is a good starting point to imagine charr migrating upstream in the autumn to spawn by digging redds in gravel to deposit their eggs, with the young fry going through basically the same development stages as portrayed in countless textbooks and wildlife films on salmon and trout. Many charr populations, especially in the Arctic, do have this form of spawning behaviour and possibly this is their preferred *modus operandi* as regards reproduction. Severe climatic or other forms of environmental marginality and competition from other species of fish (or other races of charr) can, however, result in major modification of their primary preferred option. As so often is the case with charr, the rule book goes 'right out of the window'.

In the high Arctic, charr frequently conform to the stream-spawning, redd-making mode of spawning. At lower latitudes and altitudes, in the presence of more competitive and territorial fish such as trout, charr adopt a variety of spawning options. The next preferred option is to choose spawning sites on gravel banks on the shores of the lake they inhabit. Both options may be taken up if racial division of the charr population exists. Thus we have as an example both running-water and still-water spawning charr as at Rannoch and Windermere. Spawning runs of charr are also reported in the River Tromie and the Dunachton Burn in Speyside. There appears to be a large autumnal streamward spawning migration of charr from Loch na Sealga in Wester Ross. Under pressure, for example from more competitive charr, some forms will take to spawning in the abyssal regions of a lake. This variety of options even extends to the choice of substrate for egg deposition. Charr have been recorded in Lake Torrön in Sweden as spawning on substrates of the weed *Isoetes*, as well as on stony reefs within the lake. Later damming of the lake caused the water level to

Typical charr spawning site in a hydro-electric reservoir. Draw-down has exposed the graver bank chosen. (*Per Aass*)

rise sufficiently to allow the charr ingress to previously inaccessible streams. Some of the charr then switched to 'traditional' stream spawning. This flexibility also extended to the abandonment of their original lake spawning sites to take advantage of the new gravel banks created by the expansion of the lake.

Unfortunately for my fellow charr fanatic Dr Fred Kircheis of the Fish and Wildlife Department of the State of Maine, the charr he is working with in Floods Pond did not prove so responsive to an artificial spawning site specially created for them. The charr in this lake spawn by simply dropping their eggs in the spaces between boulders on a reef that is the only known spawning site. A new reef was created, closely modelled on the original as a 'conservation safety feature', as charr are very rare in Maine. Needless to say they did not oblige their would-be saviours. Just to demonstrate further their obstinacy, some Floods Pond charr, held in an artificial stream at the University of Maine, duly spawned in running water by digging redds in the gravel!

Checking for charr eggs at Floods Pond, Maine, USA. Charr seldom appreciate the suffering of the scientists who study them! (*Fred Kircheis*)

Apart from Arctic streams, the charr which hatch after stream spawning do not form the stream-living juvenile life stages familiar in salmon or sea trout; nor generally do they develop stream resident forms as does the brown trout. On hatching they rapidly drop out of the stream to begin lake life. Little is known of their early life history in this phase. Such behaviour does convey some advantage in that charr can use temporary streams which dry out in the summer. In both still and running water charr can show strong homing instincts to their native area in much the same way that salmon do. The Windermere studies are again an excellent example. At least thirteen discrete spawning areas are recorded here. However, there can be a functional override if this is necessary, as can be seen at Lake Torrön.

The summer spawning shown by the El'Gygytgyn charr of Chukotka is not something specific to these otherwise unique fish. Spring spawning charr in Windermere are of course well-known. Summer spawning also occurs in Icelandic waters and has been reported from large Alpine lakes. This tends to happen in large water masses which have little seasonal temperature variation. Charr living permanently in abyssal regions do not experience much change in temperature in any case. If racially discrete charr groups exist in different depth zones in a lake, then spawning of one form or another might occur at most times of the year. This of course presents difficulty in the ageing of charr, especially in assigning them a first birthday from scale readings. Such a problem arose for example in the spring spawners at Windermere. Nothing like this has so far been encountered in Scottish lochs, but Loch Ness would be a likely candidate.

The success of charr in meeting the challenges of their environment is quite amazing. They themselves are part of the set of environmental conditions that allow the survival of Ferox. Some consideration of that environment is now due.

3
The Ferox and Charr Environment

W hen I first sat down to write this chapter I thought it would be a simple matter of relatively few words, well-judged extractions from learned journals and a fair sprinkling of Met. Office charts and graphs. Well, just as in Ferox fishing, nothing is as simple as it would first appear and more persistence than at first thought necessary is required to turn imagination into reality. The problem in writing a book for general readership, rather than simply describing the results of objective scientific studies, as I am more used to doing, is that subjective value judgements, based on personal experience and opinion, have to be made to guide the reader along a train of thought. This is especially true of the general and specific nature of the environment of the fish species concerned. There is substantial literature on the physical and biological characteristics of lakes and it would be impossible for me to try to précis a review of this literature of the science of limnology in the confines of this volume. A basic simple outline is all that is required so that the salient features of the Ferox and charr habitat and the differences from lowland waters can be brought to the attention of the reader.

The current demographic pattern of the British Isles dictates that the majority of readers will live in large urban conglomerations in the lowland areas of the country, especially in the southern and eastern areas of England, the central Lowlands of Scotland and the English Midlands. All these areas have no Ferox or charr populations and the human beings who live there experience a climatic and cultural regime that has little or no relation to those areas of the country where Ferox and charr abound. It is yet another facet of the classic north-west/south-east split into two 'Britains'. It is from the point of view of geological structure, biological and climatic processes, rather than the more generally accepted division of political orientation, that these two regions of our island may in large part be considered as two separate countries. The physical environment of southern England is in many ways an extension of northern France and the Low Countries, whilst Cumbria, much of Ireland and especially the Scottish Highlands are very similar to the coastal montane areas of Fennoscandia.

Northern 'ferox-charr' Britain with its rugged topography clearly shown.

This simple geographical fact is often unknown or, even worse, ignored by our bureaucrats and administrators. This is not just a matter of my Scottish bias, to which I of course freely admit. There is actually the case of Glasgow housing authorities building houses that were designed primarily for North Africa. A thorough read of a primary school geography book might have indicated that housing standards suitable for Reykjavik or Bergen might have been more appropriate. It would perhaps have saved more money in the long run and almost certainly a great deal of human misery.

It is difficult enough to attempt to convey a certain value judgement about the environment of two essentially northern types of fish largely unknown to most people, and indeed even to most anglers; the task is made doubly daunting by trying to do this in a country where people are so divorced from the reality of their own geographical and climatic position in the world. My travels in North America, Scandinavia and Russia have long convinced me that there is no group of people so maladapted as the British to their own physical environment. When visiting Norwegian farms I often came to the conclusion, after seeing double-glazed, pine-panelled sheep houses, that our Nordic cousins kept their animal stock in better conditions than we often do our senior citizens. Even in the desperate conditions of the collapse of the Soviet Union I observed better insulation standards in housing than most of the older buildings in Britain. We probably have the lowest standards in housing relative to our climatic conditions in any developed country in the world. What on earth has all this got to do with Ferox and charr? Well, simply, in a situation where human beings are the biggest threat to the survival of these fish, what chance is there of understanding the environment of the fish when the potential destroyers do not understand their own environment? So for a little longer, before I get down to describing the specific environment of the Ferox and charr, I am going to try to shed light on some of the popular misconceptions and prejudices many readers may have about northern Britain. After I have hopefully undermined these biases and prejudices the reader will be in a better frame of mind to empathise with the fish. In the process of this you will of course become aware of my own passions and prejudices. If some of you out there think 'I am having a go at you', then you would be absolutely correct. This applies especially to bureaucrats in Edinburgh and London as well of course to a certain ex-boss of mine.

My earliest memories of school geography lessons on the British Isles had, in their climatic summaries, a great deal to say about the mild equable climate derived from the influence of the Gulf Stream, or more correctly the North Atlantic Drift. Not for us the severities of Siberia or the chilling cold of Canada. I often heard my teacher lyrically waxing on about palm trees in Cornwall and January flowers in the famous gardens at Inverewe, in the north west Highlands. Somehow or other we were blessed with balmy mildness, sufficient gentle variability to make the weather a useful conversational diversion and a God-given general escape clause from climatic harshness. The reality, especially if you live a thousand feet above sea level anywhere north of Watford, is of course more than just a wee bit different.

London is as far north as the southernmost tip of Hudson's bay in that section of it known as James Bay. Glasgow, Dublin and Belfast lie in latitudes which encompass the Alaskan Panhandle. Shetland lies as far north as the southern tip of Greenland or Nunivak island in Alaska. The nearest part of the Eurasian land mass to Scotland is Norway and the nearest European country to Iceland is Scotland. These are not facts generally inculcated at school or highlighted by the perfidious weather charts of Albion, which nightly reinforce southern value judgements and dismiss blizzard conditions in the uplands as 'showers falling as snow on northern hills'.

Charr changed this perception for me and taught me to look at our position from a polar perspective. All you have to do to get a handle on this for yourself is to turn a physical map of the North Atlantic upside down. As well as being perhaps the first step in overcoming some southern-derived geopolitical and climatic prejudices, it will also provide the answer to a simple question that forced itself on me twenty years ago. That question is this. Why is a sub-Arctic/Arctic species of animal, such as charr, so common in northern Britain? The answer is simply that the environment is so suitable for it. There is very little from a charr's point of view that is marginal about its British home, very little apart from the mistakes of man that is. The same set of conditions that most of the southern-oriented population – and I include many Lowland Scots in this category – write off as being 'too cold', 'too wet' and 'too far away from the markets' are not only excellent habitat for charr and Ferox, but capable of providing the highest standard of living ever attained by human beings on planet Earth. I know because I have been in the homes and offices of Scandinavian anglers and scientists.

If we are to attain something better than an image of the British uplands as little more than a scenic idyll for Brigadoon or Wordsworth 'wonderland' summer holidays, then we have to realise that they are not some kind of failed sub-tropical region or a second-rate extension of a Mediterranean milieu. They are in fact a modified extension of the sub-Arctic and, viewed from Tromsø or Reykjavik, they are a very benevolently blessed bit of it. The same elements of windiness and wetness we tend to think as being uniquely horrible to the British mountains are, in fact, normality for millions of other northern Europeans. If Cumbria or the Grampians were islands off the coast of Norway then they would be considered very favourable places to live and work in. Their populations of charr, trout and whitefishes would be appreciated in a way that is unknown here, and their environment appreciated for what it has to offer rather than written off as something peripheral, to be enjoyed as an occasional escape from urban culture. The potential of the environment of Ferox and charr is therefore that of an oceanic sub-Arctic region and should be valued as a very special part of this climatic zone.

It is perhaps easiest to understand this climatic link if one stands in the Cairngorm car park during a January blizzard, but even in the milder western regions the coolness of the summers, the rapid drop in temperature with altitude, and the high exposure have their close counterparts in the coastal mountains of Norway and Greenland. If this situation is not realised by the mass of the present day human population then it is at least vindicated in the flora and fauna, past and present. The distribution of trees, flowers, birds and mammals all links us in many ways to other northern countries. We have felled the boreal and temperate rain forests that once clothed these islands. We have wiped out bears, wolves, sea eagles, lynx and moose. We have burned, overgrazed and denuded the hills, dales and glens. We have even deliberately removed or undermined the original human cultures of this sub-Arctic part of Britain. The terrestrial setting of the environment for Ferox and charr has been stripped and shorn of most of its brightest jewels, and we still have the nerve to tell tourists that herein lies one of the greatest wildlife treasuries of Europe. We are still blessed with an extremely interesting northern fish fauna in an environment still reasonably well intact, acid rain, hydro-electric and industrial development notwithstanding; it is worthy of a better treatment than so far meted out, and certainly worthy of a closer look.

Apart from the very obvious presence of large mountain masses, one of the main points of difference between northern and southern Britain is the presence of large glacial ribbon lakes in the former. These are the prime habitats of true Ferox in Scotland and Cumbria, though Ferox occur in lakes of different character in Ireland. Charr are also very common in these glacial ribbon lakes but, unlike Ferox, are not generally restricted to them.

Loch Rannoch – home of at least two forms of charr and some huge ferox. (*A F Walker*)

Lakes have been classified by geographers and biologists into three main types roughly analogous to the three main shapes of people recognised by the medical profession and sports scientists: the biologically richest lakes called 'eutrophic' by limnologists can be likened to short, plump people termed 'endomorphs' by nutritionists. Lakes of medium nutrient status and biological productivity are termed 'mesotrophic', and can be likened to well-built athletic humans, called 'mesomorphs'; the third main type of lake has its human counterpart in tall, thin people known as 'ectomorphs', and are known as 'oligotrophic' lakes. In this instance, however, the comparison is best limited to glacial ribbon lakes, as all oligotrophic lakes are not always of this shape and kind. These of course are only the very broadest of definitions, and the classic characters can at times, as with people, be mixed or be intermediate. Loch Lomond, for example, is like an oligotrophic glacial ribbon lake in its northern half, whilst its southern half has many characteristics of a mesotrophic lake. This physical and biological structure is in part responsible for its diverse fish population relative to other Scottish lochs.

Oligotrophic lakes, by virtue of the Greek meaning of their very name (the Greek word *oligoi* means 'few') are relatively poor in dissolved chemical nutrients, especially as many such waters in Britain and Scandinavia rest on bedrock containing little calcium. Some Irish and Alpine lakes may be somewhat better off as the underlying geology may be sedimentary rocks such as limestone. Generally, all these ice-gouged lakes are very deep, long in section relative to their surface area, and lie in mountainous regions with harsh climates. Indeed the lakes concerned are best regarded as upside down aquatic mountains retaining much of the glacial features of their origins. They are in their own way as important from a conservation perspective as a relict Arctic environment as our most treasured mountain areas.

The vast depth and mass of water many of these glacial waters contain (Loch Ness has a volume of water greater than all the freshwater bodies of England and Wales) and the climatic regime pertaining in the areas in which they occur means that the general water body never becomes very warm, and certainly remains well within the tolerance range of trout and charr. In stable, warm summers a temperature stratification occurs which results in a triple 'sandwich' of water at different temperatures. The top of this sandwich is termed the 'epilimnion'. It is about ten metres deep and seldom in Britain, apart from the immediate surface, exceeds 15° Celsius, a temperature at which trout feed actively and which charr can tolerate very well. The filling in the sandwich is the 'thermocline', a temperature transition zone where the temperature may drop by 1° Celsius per metre before reaching the layer of cold dense water known as the 'hypolimnion'. Here the temperature can easily be more than 10 degrees colder than in the epilimnion. Generally, the temperature of the hypolimnion is about 4° Celsius. This stratification can be very important in the distribution of fish and other animals and, linked with light conditions, can be responsible for considerable variations in the vertical positioning of fish during the day.

Fish are very sensitive to these temperature variations and will move to optimise their metabolic activity. In our situation this stratification can fail to develop fully during cold windy summers. It may form, then break up and then form again in an erratic way. This can have important effects on the survival of young charr and is one of the main factors giving rise to poor or good year class survival. In average years some kind of stratification will happen during the warmer months and then break down in the autumn. During strong periods of stratification the upper and lower parts do not mix to any great extent and can almost function as lakes within a lake.

In most natural situations in our glacial ribbon lakes all areas of the water generally stay at temperatures with which the charr and trout populations are comfortable. This also is generally true of oxygen concentrations in the various layers during the period of stratification. In continental climates with hot summers however, this is frequently not the case and the fish species may separate out into different temperature zones. This is part of the causation of habitat segregation between species and races of fish. Oxygen concentration levels in the hypolimnion can drop because of the decomposition of organic matter and the lack of fresh supplies from mixing with the surface layers. In our larger waters under natural conditions this is of no great concern because of the vast mass of water; however it can be a serious problem though when pollution occurs due to unnaturally large inputs of organic products and basic nutrients which can increase what is termed as the biological oxygen demand. A small degree of nutrient enrichment can actually be of benefit to charr and trout, but, if sufficiently large, can alter the environment so much that charr can no longer live in a previously excellent habitat. When or if the charr go, then it is likely also farewell to the Ferox unless an alternative prey species occurs. This may not always be a direct process. It may come about through the environment changing to favour competing species or by siltation of organic particulate matter suffocating spawning sites. The Alpine lakes, Constance, Zug and Neuchatel are thought to have suffered in this way.

Glacial ribbon lakes can be likened in a way to an Alpine garden or rockery. The rockery mimics conditions of the high mountains or the polar regions. The soil contained in a rockery represents recently originated frost-shattered debris, devoid of the richness of more favourable climes. Glacial ribbon lakes even today are not far removed from their original state and like the rockery, contain few of the nutrients that support complex plant and animal ecosystems. These harsh conditions are however tolerated by a range of species specifically adapted to this challenging milieu. The Alpine or rock garden enthusiast knows that if he fertilises the soil too much it will favour the growth of ranker weeds which will swamp out the hardy but less vigorously growing choice plants. We can even extend this comparison to the Alpine plant communities of our own mountains. The difference between our aquatic and terrestrial Arctic relict communities, in human terms, lies in our value judgements and sense of appreciation of them. There is, as my colleague Peter Maitland would say, 'a low fish appeal these days'. We would probably laugh at anyone who said that the Alpine plant communities of Ben Lawers or upper Teesdale were worthless because they are not as fertile and productive as the potato fields of Ayrshire or the grain farms of East Anglia, yet some anglers seemed to think that the glacial lakes of Ireland, Scotland and Cumbria with their simple salmonid communities needed to be stocked by a host of coarse fish species. This is like saying that a gardener's prize rock plant collection is devoid of botanic or culinary interest because there are no carrots or cabbages in it. Such a rock garden does not need cabbages or carrots. What is needed is an appreciation of the value and beauty of the special range of plants which it can grow because of the particular environment it offers. Exactly the same applies to the large glacial lakes of the north and the northern community of fish species contained in them.

Garden or lake, filberts or Ferox, the driving force of each ecosystem or individual organism is solar energy. The availability of solar energy and the basic range of nutrients determine the productivity of field, mountain, moor or lake. Radiation from the sun as light and heat facilitates the uptake of basic inorganic nutrients into the organic world of plants and animals. Even if an Arctic lake lay on sedimentary rocks rich in minerals, its potential productivity would not be realised in the same way as a less geologically blessed lake in more southern climes which had much higher energy input from the sun. Given equal energy input, then of course, basic nutrient levels would assume greater importance.

However, our large glacial lakes are not generally blessed with either. Lying on lime-poor mountains which have been scoured of much of their mineral soils by glacier action, and where climatic conditions are far from being sunny and warm, they offer a comparatively sterile environment compared to lowland eutrophic and mesotrophic waters. Their great depth of water also places a further liability on them as far as the light energy budget is concerned and one which is not met by their terrestrial equivalent. Water acts as a light filter and reflector. Reflection of light and the filtering effect of the water, as well as the suspended material it often contains in the peaty catchments of the north and west, means that sufficient light to allow plant growth reaches fewer than several metres into the water. This is of the highest significance in terms of fish production.

Fish, like all higher animals, ultimately derive their solar energy from plants. The rich weedy growths of shallow lowland lakes are not possible in glacial ribbon lakes because of the lack of light in most of the area of the lake. Only the shallow margins can sustain large leafed plants. This capacity for plant growth in the shallow margins is further limited by a lack of fine rich sediments and the powerful wave action prevalent in such waters. Modification of a natural lake to a hydro-electric reservoir can frequently wipe out the littoral plant production almost altogether. Even in the more stable conditions of the main open water mass, light capable of sustaining microscopic plants can only penetrate to a relatively short distance. Thus what is termed primary production by biologists – the initial conversion of raw chemical nutrients into living organic material by the photosynthetic action of plants – is limited in large deep waters relative to shallow ones.

The pathways of this energy and nutrient system into the living flesh of fish vary according to the main physical sub-divisions in the lake. In the shallow margins (littoral zone) the sunlight energy and nutrient supply is accessed by large rooted plants (macrophytes). These are in turn eaten either as living plant material or more often as dead material (plant detritus) by a range of insect larvae, crustaceans and molluscs. These are an extremely important food resource for fish. The littoral zone, though limited in extent because of the physical factors outlined above, is per unit area the most productive area of the lake. This qualitative difference between the littoral zone and the open water zones is not just a function of differences in the intrinsic characteristics of these zones or the deep profundal areas. In the overall rather negative description of the biological characteristics of glacial ribbon lakes, there are some positive mitigating factors. The main one is that such lakes do not operate as closed systems. The basic self-contained nutrient and energy budget is augmented from external resources, primarily derived from the surrounding landscape. The most important factor involved in this respect, especially in temperate and sub-Arctic areas, is the annual supply of leaf litter from surrounding forests in the catchment. This means that sunlight energy and nutrients from a vastly larger area than the surface of the lake can enter into the fish-producing 'equation'. The annual input of such organic material can be several tons per hectare. The benefit of this is affected by the shape of the lake concerned. Those lakes with a large shore line relative to surface area benefit most. Another important feature involved is the local terrestrial topography. Lakes surrounded by steep forested hillsides receive most benefit. On both counts this would have been exactly the case with most British glacial ribbon lakes. We have of course, because of our long love affair with pastoral hill farming, grouse moor and deer 'forest' pursuits, destroyed the forest. Somehow we have forgotten to put the price of this in the environmental resource account of our rural land use 'strategy'. We even pay vast amounts of public money through grant aid and subsidy to maintain the 'madness of the mountains'.

Though the loss is greatest in the littoral lake areas adjacent to the riparian woodland, we should also remember that many leaves find their way to the deep water zone. I remember being most struck by this during some research work on Loch Ness. Whilst trawling (not trolling as per Ferox angling) using a small beam trawl to catch bottom-dwelling fish, we frequently were brought to a halt by leaves filling the trawl, even at several hundred feet down. The open water pelagic zone receives little benefit from this type of external energy input. However, the surface of the lake does receive a positive benefit from another source, and one which most anglers will be more familiar with than the indirect processing of leaves to fish food by an invertebrate animal community. This of course is the direct 'rain' of adult insects which alights from surrounding land. It is easy to envisage a local source from immediate forest and moorland. However, a colleague of mine pointed out to me, during a description of his work on Loch Turret in southern Perthshire, that the drift of insect food to the loch was not just a local event. Insects were blown in from many miles away, often from the more fertile lowlands to the south.

These mitigating factors, even when they operate in undisturbed natural ecosystems, are extremely unlikely to raise the basic productivity to anything like that which pertains in lowland lakes in the other main physical sub-divisions mentioned above. They can and do however present a better and more optimistic potential than they are generally credited with in the British Isles at present. We should not dismiss them as merely aquatic deserts devoid of economic and ecological value. We cannot argue purely for the ground of yield of protein produced per hectare each year on a famous grouse moor that such a land use practice produces no income. We cannot even argue that gold or diamonds are valuable purely on their utilitarian benefits, though of course they do offer some important practical uses. The real value is the more abstract one; it is an intellectual concept, a value judgement by the human mind.

The same approach should be taken to the habitat of Ferox and charr. This is not to say that because of its relatively low level of biological yield that no direct economic yield can be obtained; far from it indeed. In several of the other chapters of this book I have made reference to the direct benefits offered by the harvest of charr by netting in other countries, especially in Fennoscandia. Even lakes of comparatively low productivity can produce long-term, sustainable yields of several kilograms per hectare. Given the frequently large size of the lakes involved, this can mean many tonnes of fish being captured on an annual basis. To this direct economic return can be added various indirect benefits to local rural communities. This is even more true of recreational fisheries for both Ferox and charr and other fish communities of glacial lakes. These fish communities are the 'gold' and 'diamonds' which exceed their direct first-hand value.

When scientists in specific disciplines consider the environment of the particular species that is the object of their interest, the environment that species occupies is frequently described by them purely by its physical

A beaver pond in Canada. Beavers are an integral part of the forest ecosystem and create valuable habitats for other animals – including fish.

parameters. This is correct up to a point. However, the 'life experience' of any organism in its environment also includes interactions with other living organisms. The science of ecology is built upon this precept. Scientists, being human, tend to concentrate on the immediate requirements of the species concerned. If asked to describe the nature of a forest, for example, a botanist or forester would probably give a great deal of explanation concerning tree species structure, shrub layer composition as well as constituent species and community structure of herbaceous plants etc. Probably missing in the description of the integral parts of the functioning forest would be large mammals such as wild boar and beaver. These animals might be considered a nuisance or a pest, or even helpful in their effects on the forest. They might be highly worthwhile for study by someone in another scientific discipline. Very unlikely though would be the consideration of these mammals as an integral part of the forest as much as the trees or other plants were. Beaver and boar help create the forest environment. They can alter species structure and tree density and affect the way the forest nutrient budget is allocated and distributed.

It is the same in principle in the aquatic world. Charr are part of the Ferox environment and actually, at least in most British waters, are a definitive feature of it. Both species themselves are representatives of a special set of northern fish species that are characteristic of the glacial origin of our upland environment and their very presence makes that physical environment function in the way it presently does, and assigns a special value judgement to it in terms of its conservational value to society.

The great biological divide of the aquatic environment of northern and southern Britain is well highlighted by many features, not the least of which is the species composition of their naturally occurring fish communities and the origins and distribution history of those fish communities. It is a natural distribution much obscured now by introductions made by human agency, deliberate and accidental. The present, as we all know but tend to forget, is a function of the past. Two of the most salient features of that past in terms of our fish communities are the occurrence of the Ice Ages and the creation of Britain as an island off the coast of Europe as a feature of the deglaciation process of the current inter-glacial period.

At the peak of glaciation it is very likely that all fish species were wiped out on the mainland north of where London now stands. Around the coast of the ice-free areas and running into the rivers of those regions were groups of fish species known as euryhaline fishes. These are characterised by their capacity to tolerate water of widely varying degrees of salinity. Included in this group of fishes are many salmonid species, including salmon itself, trout, charr, smelt, Coregonid whitefishes, shad, eel and various species of sticklebacks. The other main group of fishes, known as stenohaline species can survive only in fresh water and generally require much warmer conditions to thrive. These species include most of the carp family and other non-game fishes. Both sets of fishes could only re-invade as the ice melted and conditions warmed up. The warming-up process, however, caused what is now the North Sea to fill in, and also established the salt water barrier of the English channel. The longer persistence of the glaciers or peri-glacial conditions in northern Britain, the comparatively early isolation from the European mainland, and the north-east/south-west alignment of the main mountain ranges meant that the northern fish fauna was derived mainly from the limited range of euryhaline species. The stenohaline species were themselves prevented from invading even southern Britain from the freshwater drainage basin of Europe by the ingress of the sea. Thus both groups of fishes are not so diverse in Britain compared to continental regions. The natural fish species of the north and west of Britain is almost solely derived from the limited range of euryhaline species.

This relative paucity of species is certainly not poverty in terms of biological interest. The distribution and origins of these euryhaline species leaves a living record in our northern lakes of the most dramatic features of the effects of glaciation on the distribution of fishes. Of particular interest in this respect is the distribution of the whitefish species pollan and powan. There are only five locations in Ireland where the former occurs, and six on mainland Britain where the latter is found. This is a very restricted distribution compared to charr and trout. The Swedish scientist, Professor Sven Segerstrale, put forward the hypothesis that this was due to the lesser tolerance of pollan and powan of full salinity seawater compared to charr and trout. There was only limited opportunity at certain periods of glaciation for these fish to emigrate along the low salinity water at the margin of the glacier front. Emigration was from a giant freshwater refugial lake in western Russia. The distribution of whitefish coincides quite closely with certain relict invertebrate species, especially in the Irish loughs. The recent advances in genetic methods of comparing fish stocks confirmed that pollan were in fact the same species, *Coregonus autumnalis*, as the Siberian cisco. Pollan are not found in England or Scotland, but interestingly Ennerdale in Cumbria contains the glacial relict shrimp *Mysis relicta* and a race of charr which seems to be genetically distinct from other Cumbrian lakes. Considering that the whitefish species are so rare it is interesting that we have charr and powan co-existing in Haweswater and Loch Eck, and charr and pollan in Lough Erne. The distribution and ecology of charr and white fish in Fennoscandia suggests that the whitefish have a negative effect on charr, primarily through competition for plankton. Geological studies indicate that at a certain period of glacial history the Baltic was a freshwater lake. The altitudinal limit of the natural distribution of whitefish coincides very well with the ancient shore line. Charr are only common above this zone, having been 'replaced' by the coregonid fishes below it, or forced to occupy a different niche. Our glacial upland lakes then contain a very special fish fauna indeed, both in content and in combination of species, in some ways paralleling the botanic value of the Alpine plants of Ben Lawers.

The species complex of any given water is not just a matter of biogeographical or academic interest. It has a major feedback loop to the basic environment of the lake and the basic energy and nutrient flow mentioned earlier in the chapter. The plankton communities of fishless lakes are very different from otherwise identical lakes which contain fish. In the former, the plankton community is dominated by comparatively large, highly palatable species of animal plankton known as Cladocera, examples being creatures such as daphnia, the well-known water flea. If plankton-feeding fish are introduced to such a previously fishless lake these are very rapidly and selectively preyed upon; the result is a change in the structure of the animal plankton community. This change often manifests itself in the dominance of smaller, less palatable plankton animals known as copepods; prominent among these are species of the genera Cyclops and Diaptomus. Various species of fish have different capacities to harness this resource. Charr are better at it than trout, but inferior to most whitefish species.

The presence of an effective plankton-feeding fish can have important effects on the level of plant plankton production as well as the plankton production affecting the feeding potential of the fish in the first place. It is a delicate balance between bottom up and top down interactions. Basic nutrient and sunlight energy levels dictate the production of plant plankton. This in turns provides the source of nourishment for animal plankton which later forms the food of open water species for fish. However, the different forms of animal plankton can affect the structure of the plant plankton through predation and the fish do the same to the animal plankton; the system is not static and operates within the laws of thermodynamics in several ways.

One of these variables is the presence of a fish predator and here we return to the Ferox that is the subject of this book. Ferox have their own top down effect on the very system that produces them. They are proven effective fish predators that can affect the structure of the prey fish that support them. The Norwegian scientists Terje Sandlund and Tor Nesje studied the effects on the lower parts of the ecosystem in lakes and suggested that Ferox have an important role in the structure of plant and animal plankton communities and in maintaining high water quality. Ferox are a part of the living flow of energy in the lakes they inhabit. They can in a limited biological sense affect the very nature of that habitat.

They are part of the totality of the experience for anglers venturing out on the glacial stage of a past era, an era probably set to return in the not too distant future. That environment is a very special one in its own right. It is a treasure to equal the glories of the mountains which surround it. It has to be judged from a polar perspective and appreciated its own in merits and terms. In coming to terms with it in both a sporting and biological basis, one can sample the pleasures of hunters of Ferox past and present. If one cannot come to terms with it then it is best to leave it alone.

4

The Hunters and Their Methods – Cro-Magnon no more!

'Trolling for giant trout is the very acme of rod-fishing.' Thus wrote Sir John Colqhoun of Luss in 1880 in his book *The Moor and the Loch*. This book is required reading in my opinion for any would-be Ferox angler. Just as the aerial combat tactics of modern air forces are based on the lessons learned by the 'knights of the air' of the Great War despite the massive advance of technology since then, so is modern day Ferox angling similarly indebted to the pioneers of yesteryear. Having recognised Sir John's contribution we should also not forget others like T. Speedy, T.T. Stoddart, W.C.G. St John and P.D. Malloch, who all, through their experiences and writings, enhanced our sporting repertoire. Just as importantly we should not forget the unsung contribution of local people who acted as ghillies and mentors to those more literate, but not necessarily more knowledgeable, about Ferox angling than themselves. Specific terms of description for various forms of trout, including Ferox, are either in Gaelic (Scots and Irish) or derived from this language. 'Gillaroo', 'Sonaghen' and 'Duermain' were brought to the appreciation of our sporting ancestors by way of the observational skills and local knowledge of people whose experience is not often recognised. Ferox were not 'discovered' by these above-mentioned 'giants' of angling's literary lore; they were probably known to local residents for thousands of years.

Raising Ferox angling to the acme of rod-sport was, however, largely a creation of these Victorian and Edwardian gentlemen, and their success in bringing the status of catching a Ferox in the sporting culture of the Highlands on a par with bagging a stag or salmon is a testimony both to their angling skills and to their literary advocacy of this branch of angling. Speaking from a totally biased position, I would of course agree with Sir John's view. Ferox angling is for me the acme of angling activity. I would ask the reader though to listen not only to the experiences of men like Sir John, but also to defer to disciples of more recent days who recognise that the 'acme of angling' can be an agonising pastime. No matter how good you become, or how often you try, you are never going to catch massive numbers of fish. In the process you will alternatively approach hypothermia, heat-stroke, exhaustion, desiccation and drowning. So if your pleasure comes from catching hordes of tame rainbows put in for the pecuniary advantage of fish-farmers, or bagging huge hauls of mackerel whilst on holiday, my advice to you regarding Ferox angling is – don't even start! Whether accepting or rejecting the information and advice offered within these pages, one can do no better than take heed once more of Sir John's thoughts: 'Neither rules nor practice will make a man an angler unless he has a turn for it.' Ferox angling requires a ruthless determination to overcome the vicissitudes of climate, fish, 'psychology' and providence, though luck can obviously play a part, and again Sir John recognised this in another timeless quotation: 'Sometimes, in spite of all the odds, the bungler gains the day.' There is still, however, no substitute for sound preparation, planning and serious application.

That preparation begins within yourself. The most important factor in Ferox angling is your mind. If progress is to be made in this branch of our sport then you must develop a philosophy. This Ferox philosophy is not an easy one to master, and the known difficulty of developing it helped assuage the concerns of my fellow members of the Ferox-85 Group, who were worried that I would give away the hard-won nitty-gritty of how to go about catching a Ferox. The nitty-gritty is of course an ingredient of this chapter, but, as with the fish, takes some effort to obtain.

This is the chapter that I most wanted to write and no doubt many of you wanted to read. Some of you may have despaired of the scientific passages in the early chapters and skipped these to rush to this one in order to learn as quickly as possible how to wangle out a whopper in ten seconds. In that case you have just made your first mistake in Ferox angling, and most of you will subsequently have given up after the first or second ten-hour blank day. My favourite summary for this situation is that it will feel like a brain-numbing, bum-numbing fishless eternity. Those who survive this will be relatively few in number and will thoroughly deserve their fish. Remember that you are after a wild fish in a wild environment and catching it is a far cry from the pursuit of some hand-reared 'dumbo' that has never had to hunt for its dinner in its life. It is no coincidence that two past captors of wild rod-caught record brown trout were scientists as well as anglers. Dr Niall Campbell is in fact a leading authority on the ecology of Ferox and Alistair Thorne has twenty-five years of scientific work in Highland lochs under his belt. Knowing about the fish is not just an academic exercise, it is an essential ingredient of the philosophical approach to Ferox angling and a major component in avoiding the negative experiences outlined above. So if you have not read the early chapters already, pour yourself another dram and start again.

Since your mind is the most important part of your Ferox 'tackle box' then you should use your brain to think through the schedule of your approach. I have put forward the case in the early chapters that the Ferox phenomenon is basically a feature of the sub-Arctic environment. This means that if you are after an Arctic animal in an Arctic environment you are going to experience the main feature of that zone – the raw climate. Since the British uplands lie in a highly oceanic part of the sub-Arctic, it's going to be a penetratingly damp and stormy experience.

Before you think about even the smallest item in your tackle box you have to think about your protective clothing. There is no point in holding a reel or rod that is the latest piece of computer-designed, laser-crafted technology when you cannot turn the handle because your fingers are so numb. What is the point of dreaming of the fish of a lifetime if, when the dream comes true, you cannot bear to move because you are soaked to the skin by melting sleet running down your neck? This is not just a matter of comfort but of safety. A good flotation suit or buoyancy aid can keep you alive as well as dry and warm. There is a vast array of suitable clothing available today in both natural and man-made fibres. Personally I prefer musk ox-fibre, but you don't meet many musk ox in Britain these days. (I am working on a musk ox re-introduction project at present with a colleague. We see Ferox anglers as a possible market outlet!) In the meantime avail yourself of: a pair of chest waders; at least two layers of leg and footwear underneath; three layers of upper body clothing, two preferably of wool; and an outer windproof and

Ferox fishing can be fun if equipment and protective clothing are up to the rigours of a 'sub-arctic session'. (*The Scotsman*)

waterproof anorak or suit. Top this off with a hat, scarf and gloves. I cannot stress the importance of this preparation enough. You are going to be 'stuck' in a boat for hours at a stretch with limited movement to warm you up. In any kind of wind, even at a temperature of five or ten degrees Celsius, this can be awful if you are not ready for it. Ferox angling takes up lots of rod hours in wet and windy conditions. If you cannot hold out then you will not catch fish; it is as simple as that. This protective clothing need not be especially expensive or top of the designer range; Ferox are not influenced by sartorial elegance. Garments that allow your body to breathe are not necessary as serious physical exertion is limited to the start of the day and its end. Personally I do not rate highly those expensive brand-name waxed cotton jackets beloved of the 'Sloane Rangers'. You never seem to be comfortable in these clothes, and even on a dry day they seem to exert a dank, restrictive influence.

Further to these external factors your preparation should also take care of the inner self in the form of sufficient food and hot drinks. Stainless steel flasks are a worthwhile investment. Take more food and drink than you think will be necessary. Needing it and not having it is much less preferable than the reverse. This does not apply to alcohol and, fond as I am of a good malt whisky or real ale myself, it is best to limit alcoholic beverages in the interests of safety. Leave the celebratory or compensatory inebriation to the shore-based après-Ferox cultural exchange for non-drivers!

Coldness and wetness are your main adversaries on most days, but please remember, especially if you are fair-skinned as I am, to take adequate protection from the sun. Even on cold days the sun can still burn your skin, aided by the reflected light from the water and the desiccating effects of the wind. Woolly hat and sunglasses are sometimes the odd-looking order of the day, but together with UV barrier creams they can keep you in fine fettle for a Ferox. This weather warning is a matter of personal experience of either coming in frozen to the marrow or with a face like Dennis the Menace's backside after parental punishment. Once at Loch Laggan a Ferox 85 Group member who initially ridiculed my 'Nanook of the North' approach gladly accepted a spare anorak after a fight with a Ferox in a sleet storm. This, if nothing else, proved that the fish was happier in freezing weather than he was. Another few minutes and the fish would have won. The soundness of the above advice will become distressingly obvious should you decide to ignore it. Leave the macho stuff to Clint Eastwood or Sylvester Stallone, but even these guys would not make it in the west Highlands if they forgot their midge repellent. If the Ferox are fickle, you can always rely on a million bites from these insects.

You are still a long way from getting properly prepared for the fray. The mainstay of Ferox angling is trolling (more correctly trailing) from a boat. Though there are other useful methods, about which I'll say more later in the chapter, it is this one which will be most likely to get you that fish of your angling career. Any old boat will simply not do. You need a boat that can allow you to stand up broadside on to a stiff wind and take five-foot waves head on. Remember that some of the lochs or loughs you will be fishing on are nearly as long as the English Channel is wide at its narrowest point, and, like this sea channel, they can get dangerously rough. Many of the boats available for hire on Highland lochs are sadly not up to the job. Our Irish and Scandinavian cousins seem to be much better prepared. Frequently the outboards associated with these boats receive only peremptory maintenance, and usually are the type with an integral tank that has the annoying habit of running dry just when things are at their worst. The boat set-up is usually geared for standard loch-style flyfishing, involving a short journey to and from favoured drifts. What is really required for trolling is a fifteen- or sixteen-foot coble, preferable with a cuddy, and a well-maintained outboard with a remote tank. The outboard should be of six to fifteen horsepower (remember, you are on a fishing trip, not an ego trip). The above advice is not just about comfort or efficiency, it is also about staying alive. As a professional fish biologist I can tell you that the distribution area of Ferox does not include Davy Jones's locker.

My own preference is for an Orkney Longliner or Arran boat. If you think the open cabin might interfere with your flyfishing then you would be correct. Forget about this 'escape clause' and become more relentless. A single-minded obsessive approach is vital for success. One day Ferox fever might well be classified as a form of psychosis; just enjoy it in the meantime and think more about the tackle required.

Apart from the biological myths associated with Ferox, the most sheer and utter nonsense is talked about the tackle and methods required to capture them. This tends to vary from the extreme position that the old heavyweight Victorian tackle 'is what you really need' to the other extreme of the technological 'gear freak' approach with the latest in-built satellite tracking systems; 'converted' carp and pike anglers are the worst in this latter respect, and traditional salmon anglers in the former. The truth, as I see it, lies in a pragmatic and practical blending of both viewpoints. Going over the top is not economically worthwhile, or more likely to get you more fish. Watching an echo-sounder screen, though sometimes very helpful, is much less interesting than sharing a joke with your companions or observing the local wildlife. You may even miss out on witnessing the varied mating behaviour of humans on shore-based Highland holidays. Yes, it is amazing what a Ferox troller sees on an outing! The strangest thing that has happened to me on a trolling trip was being observed by a Cherokee and an Apache standing in the Black Wood of Rannoch. On reflection I think it was getting a bit too quiet at the time! Our North American visitors were promptly asked to join us for an evening meal to mull over comparisons of Ferox and lake-trout (actually a species of piscivorous charr) fishing techniques.

The question most frequently asked of me by the average 'Ferox tyro' is, 'what reel and rod do I need?' Well at this stage I usually recommend deferment of this consideration until much later. Some rods and reels are of course much more useful than others for particular purposes, but the fact is that most of the vast range of carp, salmon and pike rods available on the market can be used very successfully. There is no need to be fussy or faddy or spend a vast fortune on the latest factory or hand-built creation. As an example of this I can relate that the second largest Ferox caught by the Ferox 85 Group, in its pursuit of the British rod-caught record, was a Loch Arkaig fish of 17lb taken on an eight-foot pike spinning rod, bought in a closing down sale, and an old dilapidated salmon fly reel loaded with Kingfisher No.3 line. Not that this tackle would be the primary choice of course, but it worked. It worked because the 'business end' was equal to the task. That

Waiting for the rod to go round in a pulsating curve. (*The Scotsman*)

business end was the last three feet of line containing the bait, its mounting, the sinker and anti-kink device.

Put thoughts of rod and reel aside for a moment and reflect upon the parts of your outfit that are responsible for your initial and only direct contact with the Ferox – the hooks. The majority of hooks on the market are not up to the job, especially a well-known Norwegian brand. My late friend and colleague Bruce Macauslan thought, after thirty years of experience of trolling, that the best thing to do with this particular brand of hooks was to consign them to the scrap merchant along with your Seagull engine. Basically what is required is a well-tempered and very sharp hook with a short barb and a short distance from barb to point. In descending order of choice, Bruce's and the later experience of the Ferox-85 Group indicate that Partridge Outpoint trebles are the best, then Eagle Claw Laser Sharp and Kamasan as a poor third. On buying new lures or spoons we now change the trebles on them as a matter of course. There is no need to opt for the very heavy wire gauge varieties and, indeed, these may ruin the action of finely balanced lures such as the Rapala. The needle-eye hooks in the range, though fine for tube flies and dead-bait traces, are also not suitable for lures. These quality hooks are relatively expensive, but what is the point of begrudging a few pence per hook extra and then spending tens or hundreds of pounds on a fancy reel or flashy rod? It is the combined experience of Ferox-85 Group members that more Ferox are lost because of failed hooking than breakage of line or rod. Spending slightly more cash is preferable to spending more time wondering about what might have been. I know because I have 'been there'.

A word of warning though is required with regard to both the Partridge Outpoint and the Eagle Claw hooks. These hooks are very efficient and very sharp indeed. As well as securing an extra sound grip in a fish, they can also do so to you. If you are unfortunate enough to impale your digits on them, then the normal medical rule applied to standard round-bend hooks is not appropriate. Trying to push the hook through the flesh and then cutting off the barb in the normal manner will only result in embedding the hook more securely because of the inherent angle of the hook. This is based on personal and practical experience in a doctor's surgery in Connel Ferry. It was small compensation to me to know how really effective these hooks can be. It was a nice excuse later, however, for some twenty-year-old single malt 'general anaesthetic'.

Much the same high quality approach needs to be taken to the line used. Beginners tend to make two basic mistakes in choosing line. One is to buy a bulk supply of cheap nylon monofil, and the other is to buy too high a breaking strain. Our preference in Ferox-85 lies for quality lines such as Berkeley Trilene Big Game, Maxima and braided Dacron. You are living in fantasy land if you think you will need anything in excess of 20lb breaking strain in any of them. We generally choose lines between 10 and 15lb breaking strain. Ferox are doughty fighters as you might happily find out before long, but they are not more likely pound-for-pound to break your line than a large salmon or pike. Another important factor for consideration here is not to become stuck in your ways. New lines offering suppleness, low stretch (very important for secure hooking at very long distances) and small diameter relative to line strength are constantly coming on the market. A persistent search for improvement should be a constant part of your approach.

The best quality line is of no avail if you do not think about what is going to happen to it during the long relentless hours of trolling you have committed yourself to. If you have opted for a wobbled dead bait, spinning lure or bait which revolves on its longitudinal axis, then you will require an anti-kink system. Again this simple fact, well-known to anglers of the past, is little considered by their modern-day counterparts. The central core of the system is a ball-bearing swivel 'backed up' by attachment to a 'half-moon', Wye or Hillman lead, which also serves as a depth control mechanism. For shallow water or immediate sub-surface trolling a plastic or aluminium 'half-moon' can be substituted. I sometimes attach a second ball-bearing swivel at the head of the bait or lure. Ball-bearing swivels are, like the high quality hooks required, more expensive than ordinary barrel swivels. They are well worth paying for, not only to allow you to fish more efficiently, but also to preserve your sanity. A 'bird's nest' of kinked line is not the easiest start to the day, especially if a swarm of midges arrives to keep you company.

The positioning of the anti-kink lead above bait or lure is not too critical. We usually allow about three to four feet of trace between lure and lead. Ferox do not appear to be fussy about it. We have caught fish of up to 12lb with only eighteen inches between the bait and sinker. It is not necessary to use wire traces for Ferox for, although they have a deadly dentition for the capture of charr, they lack the 'knife edge' sides to the teeth found in pike. Wire traces are in fact a liability. We have lost several substantial fish because of kinking, despite the claims of the manufacturers' labels attesting to the suppleness of the product. The braided wire that forms the actual spinning or wobble tackle is usually enough if a pike does take instead of a Ferox. Do not curse if this happens for Highland pike fight like hell, so it is just as well to accept and enjoy the experience. A good pike is a lot better than a blank day. Pike that have been feeding on charr or trout in Highland lochs tend to taste better than their lowland cousins consuming roach and perch, and make an excellent meal themselves. My friend Bruce Macauslan was of the old Scottish school of thought who placed pike in the category of vermin. His actual term for them was 'GSB' – green slimy b***s! Pike are not native to the Highlands and are not a feature of the natural ecology of this region. Contrary to the popular mythology of the pike-angling sub-culture with its mores developed in a totally different set of environmental and cultural backgrounds, pike living in Highland lochs do not live solely off sick and injured fish or younger pike. They are avid consumers of healthy charr and trout as well as salmon smolts. Nonetheless they are still worthy angling adversaries and can add spice to the day.

Anti-kink leads are not strictly necessary if using most plugs or Rapala-type lures, and the makers sometimes make recommendations about avoiding weights up trace. Some lures seem more affected than others, but we generally have found that no serious impairment of action occurs, especially with jointed lures. It is worth a bit of trial and error in allowing lures to achieve the depths most cannot reach. We once caught a double-figure Ferox using two three-ounce leads up trace of a single-bodied lure, so we know of at least one fish which thought the action satisfactory.

The choice of bait or lure is at one and the same time the most pleasant and the most frustrating features of Ferox fishing. Basically it is the vast range on the market that is the problem. Compared to the high point of Ferox fishing in the last century we are completely spoiled for choice; so much so in fact that we tend to forget that our Victorian predecessors did extremely well using a much more limited selection compared to the cornucopia of choice we have in modern times. We should not lose sight however of the efficacy of some of their tried and tested techniques. Unfortunately many of the old lures of repute are no longer in production. However, this is a blessing in disguise, for it can provide a stimulus to search around for old tackle and to collect books giving advice on home production. Remember that you are going to have six months of the year when the law prohibits trout fishing. Make the best of it and improve your 'arsenal'. To enter the world of Ferox fishing is to enter a captivating all year round sub-culture. First to notice this will, if you are married, be your wife and family. Glossy and exotic tackle magazines from America (basically toy catalogues for men who know that they have never grown up and are not embarrassed about it), will probably be placed by your spouse in the same category as hard-core pornography. I wonder if the redoubtable Mary Whitehouse ever received any letters from wives complaining that their husbands were more interested in the colour variations of the Arbogast whopper stopper lure (yes there really is such a thing) than in their latest, expensive haute couture?

Pride of place in artificial lures chosen by our Ferox-angling ancestors was taken by the 'phantom minnow', or, to use Sir John Colqhoun's expression, the 'phantom parr'. Made from treated fabric with a metal head replete with spinning vanes, the skill and artistry of the makers produced a very realistic lure that imitated a young trout, salmon or minnow very convincingly indeed. The lure has a very enticing fluttering spin, even on the slowest retrieve or troll. It was also a deadly lure for salmon and pike. I feel sorry for the generation of anglers that followed post-war 'baby boomers' such as myself, because it went off the stock list of tackle shops in the late 1960s. I have a secret supply but, needless to say, I'm not going to reveal its whereabouts within these pages. Another very effective lure in the revolving artificial minnow family was the rubber or leather wagtail Devon. To some extent this has been replaced by what is known euphemistically as the 'flying condom' – really a 'species' of blade spinner. Luckily, Ferox anglers can still avail themselves of a still surviving member of the Devon dynasty, in the form of the quill minnow. Those made from real quill feathers are to my mind preferable to the modern plastic version, which is still however an excellent choice. Unfortunately these lures only come in sizes under four inches and, bearing in mind the prey size preferences of Ferox outlined in the first chapter, this is something of a drawback. However, this did not prevent the capture of large Ferox in the past and they are a useful addition to the tackle box. Standard Devon minnows are of course useful too, especially those with a flat side section, imparting something of the flutter of the phantom. All these above lures, apart from the blade spinner, are guaranteed more than any other to kink your line in a short time if you do not take the steps, mentioned earlier, to prevent it.

Blade spinners, most familiar to the fishing fraternity in the form of the famous Mepps spoon, do not seem to have been in general use last century or early in this one. Exceptions to this were the 'vibro spoon' and 'kidney bar spoon'. I have to admit that I am not convinced of their general effectiveness for Ferox, though they are certainly proven catchers of smaller trout. However, this applies only to the 'normal' form of the 'Mepp'. Those which come attached to synthetic fish are very effective indeed. Fortunately they come in sufficiently large sizes to come into the reckoning as prime prey size for Ferox. My simple advice on this type of lure is: get some in. Blade spinners also have a very important indirect use in Ferox. By removing the treble hook you can then use them as in-line attractors attached varyingly at the head of the fish, midway between bait and lead, or attached directly to the half-moon lead. Some examples of sample rigs are shown on page 84/85. In this system the ball-bearing swivel is still essential even though the blade spinner will not in itself cause kinking. Mepps have actually provided, unintentionally but happily enough for us, an almost complete package in the form of the Mepps 'Lusox'. This lure has a weighted head with an articulating metal bar. The bar allows easier retrieval if caught on the bottom, whilst the lure provides weight and attraction at one and the same time. The specially fluted blade appears to be highly attractive to trout and spins at very slow retrieval speeds. By removing the treble hook and attaching a split ring you can then add a ball-bearing swivel to complete the set-up. The vibrations from the blade of this lure seem to be especially effective in tempting Ferox to strike at the bait behind. Strangely few hits occur on the lure itself. It may seem strange at first to use this method, but it is very effective indeed and I thoroughly recommend it without hesitation. This is part of the nitty-gritty promised earlier in the chapter.

Perhaps the greatest difference in the 'lure armoury' of the late twentieth-century Ferox angler compared to his equivalents in the nineteenth century and early twentieth century is in the choice of lures based on the principle of a front mounted vane providing 'live action' and diving capacity. The term 'plug' does not appear completely apt here to describe the incredible diversity developed in particular by North American and Scandinavian tackle manufacturers. The name Rapala has become synonymous with this lure in the way Hoover has with vacuum cleaners. There is no doubt about the success of these lures and such is their vast range of shape, colour and action, not to mention a highly diverse and occasionally amusing nomen-clature, that a separate glossary would be required to encompass them all. They probably represent the greatest advance in terminal tackle for Ferox in two hundred years, and your tackle box should be well adorned with them. I warn you, however, that you will probably fall foul of their attractiveness even more than the Ferox will. A compulsion develops akin to that of the heavy drinker or smoker, though in this case it is more of a wealth risk than a health risk. In Britain the available range of these lures, though vast, pales to insignificance compared to the USA or Canada. This is more than can be said of the price. On both counts I would recommend that the interested reader contacts Cabela's, 13th Ave., Sydney, Nebraska or L.L. Bean, Free-port, Maine. Can anyone in the British tackle industry please tell us why exactly the same brand of tackle, made in the same foreign factories, is substantially cheaper (including transport and customs charges) to buy from American or Canadian catalogues? Are there sharks in the British tackle industry ripping chunks out of our wallets? Even allowing for the above mentioned duty and transport charges, substantial bargains can be had. Never miss a chance to stock up if you are lucky enough to have friends on holiday on the other side of the Atlantic on whom you can impose, and certainly not if you can go there yourself. A visit to an American tackle shop, even a modestly sized one, is the adult angler's equivalent of a trip to Santa Claus land. When you see what is on offer and at what price, you will wish we had all gone to the Boston Tea Party.

I cannot admit to a comprehensive knowledge of the performance of this vast array of lures, but more than a decade of Ferox angling myself and the experience of fellow fanatics point out some useful tips in the choice of lures of this type. Jointed Rapalas seem to be particularly attractive to Ferox. The most effective colours tend to be silver and black, gold and black and 'rainbow parr'. The ABU trout-coloured Hi-Lo plug is also very successful. Lures with an in-built coating of guanine, the protein which gives the shiny silvery colour of salmon smolts, are a good choice. Lure size also matters, and even small trout will attack large Rapalas. On only two known occasions have trout over 5lb been taken on lures less than three inches long by our members.

There are two basic faults with opting for these lures. The passion for collection and experiment leads to a surfeit of lures being bought and a too frequent desire to change them instead of just being relentless with proven contenders. The other basic fault, especially in single-bodied lures, is bad hooking success. Fish can get a purchase on the body and use it as lever to extricate the hooks. This can be circumvented by not only changing to a superior quality of hook, as outlined earlier, but also by replacing the normal split ring attachment with oval types. It is worth the peace of mind for such small extra effort. In selecting plug-type lures you should also bear in mind that the well-known salmon lure – the 'Kynoch Killer', is also very effective for Ferox.

I am not a frequent user of metal spoons for Ferox, but there is no doubt about their historical track record in catching huge trout. My personal preference is for long slim spoons based on the famous Jim Vincent 'Norfolk Broads' pike spoons, the most famous of which is of course the well-known 'toby'. The main disadvantage of spoons is their poor hooking ability. This again can be countered by the use of oval split rings or the use of an extra round one at the business end. The angler is again spoiled for choice here; we now even have available laser-printed fish-holograph spoons. The fact is that again it is not worth the bother getting too fussy. Home-made spoons are a useful and much cheaper alternative whose construction makes the winter evenings pass pleasantly enough. Table-spoons cut on their long-itudinal axis have an enticing action. Don't forget that spoon, fork and knife handles also make good lures when bent correctly. Jumble sales are a good raw material source and may save the kitchen cutlery from disappearing. Salmon and pike sizes of spoons are ideal for Ferox and are always useful additions to the armoury.

Plugs, spoons, blade spinners and assorted artificial minnows; all fine and efficient lures fit to fish for a Ferox, but when I get down to making choices about my approach the experiences of my youth in trout and pike fishing in the hard-fished waters around Glasgow stick in my mind. The words of Sir John Colquhoun also reverberate once more in my ears. Both concern the use of a natural bait in preference to an imitation. One of the strongest memories I have of my early teenage years, apart from my first illicit hangover, was watching a mature gentleman fishing the natural minnow for trout at the mouth of the Covie Burn as it enters the River Avon, itself a tributary of the Clyde. I had been spinning metal Devons all morning in the falling spate to no great avail, when the chap in question came along as I was having lunch and in rapid form took five sizeable trout from the same pool that I had just blanked on. In response to my youthful curiosity he explained his tackle and tactics. I don't know who this bloke was, but I owe him a great deal. Much of what he told me that day has been employed successfully in the pursuit of Ferox, including the capture of the British record. It was basically only a matter of scaling up, with some simple modification, the Archer or Aerial tackle for minnow fishing. To this knowledge was added the later lessons taught to me by an émigré Pole, fishing in the Forth and Clyde canal, on the techniques of using a wobbled dead fish for pike. Using a small perch or roach I and my friends frequently caught pike, where those using spoons and spinners failed.

Like so much in angling life there was nothing new under the sun. In 1880 Sir John Colqhoun wrote the following passage: 'Those who prefer the phantom minnow or parr to natural bait will find the brown phantom best for Loch Layghal, though for Shin, the green is most deadly. For my own part, I prefer the natural bait to either. A phantom enthusiast assured me that in his hand the apparition had quite beat the natural bait, until he fastened false gills to the latter, when they were about equal. This showed pretty well that the real bait had no fair play until the gills were stuck on. Of course, if anyone is not a fisherman enough to make the natural bait spin true without gills, the phantom must then beat it. We had plenty of phantom parrs, but when the hour of trial came, both of us declined the honour of precedence, as each was persuaded that the substance was better than the shadow.' The last sentence is the most telling of an insightful passage of piscatorial prose. It rings in my ears every time I think my fingers are too numb to rig up a fresh bait in an April blizzard, or when I can't keep my eyes awake in the 'simmer dim' of a summer solstice session. Proper preparation and practice for the employment a dead bait is admittedly much more of a 'palaver' than simply tying on a spoon or plug, but to my mind and to those of other members of the Ferox-85 Group it is the prime method to plump for. If you decide not to master its intricacies then I am afraid that you will be operating with one hand tied behind your back. All artificial lures are an attempt to deceive the fish totally. Not so with the use of a real fish. You are actually presenting the predator with its primary prey. The deception only covers fooling the Ferox into believing this is its live prey, and sometimes even this is not necessary.

The first problem to solve of course is getting the supply of bait. This is not always as easy as it seems. Few of us have a ghillie to procure baits from a local burn in the way the Victorian upper classes had. Charr are even harder to come by. Luckily Ferox will readily accept substitutes, even sea fish. Sprats or whitebait make an excellent choice for waters where the Ferox run between 5- and 10lb. Herring, a favourite of last century, are useful for larger Ferox, though they have a tendency to become soft very quickly. Smelt, dace and grayling are baits par excellence in every sense; tough and durable as well as shiningly attractive. These days of home freezers make laying in a stock much easier than in the past. Fresh wild fish are much tougher than most frozen fish or fish obtained from hatcheries. Remember that if you are using wild trout in Scotland there is a legal requirement that these should exceed nine inches in length. It is permissible to spend a few days flyfishing to obtain bait provided this is genuine and not merely an anxious deferment of the moment of pursuit of our magnificent quarry. Preserved fish are a much lower priority though salted ones are fine.

Thinking about using herring-sized baits for trout fishing is a difficult mental obstacle to overcome, especially if you have not read that section of chapter one which deals with the food preferences of Ferox. Ignore your doubts, the cynicism and ridicule of your friends and bash on regardless. Even experienced trollers sometimes have doubts about this. My late friend Bruce Macauslan was a classic example. Being initially a 'lure freak' he often cast aspersions on the size of the baits I used. Once at Loch Arkaig, on a Ferox outing with him, I caught a trout of three pounds using a half-pound fish as bait. When I asked him if he thought my bait too big *now*, he came up with an unprintable colloquial reply to the effect that he believed that the Ferox's interest in the bait had more to do with its sexual proclivities than with hunger. Over the years I have been faced with similar credulity problems from other anglers and you will encounter similar prejudice no doubt. Persistence against this prejudice will have its reward. The look on a cynic's face when you are successful is worth all the mockery. There is no better example of this than the occasion of the inaugural gathering of the Ferox-85 Group at Loch Quoich in June 1985. After four days trolling in what amounted to the only hot summer weather of the year, I was thoroughly ragged by my friends for persisting with large dead baits in the face of a total blank. We then switched venue to Loch Arkaig where the rest of the team abandoned me on the shore to continue the battle, and they took the boat to go flyfishing. I had the good fortune to catch a ten inch trout which I then rigged on a wobble tackle. As I was picked up on the return boat journey I asked Bruce Macauslan for a couple of passes through a known Ferox 'mark'. The result was the capture of an 11lb Ferox which proved my point. My insufferable vengeful arrogance on the way home is now a legendary feature of our social gatherings. They deserved it of course as much as I did my fish. So do not be put off by ridicule or early failure.

Once the mental barrier of using baits that dwarf most artificial lures is overcome, you then have to get down to thinking about the rigging methods to ensure effective presentation. There are basically two approaches here: the spin like a Devon minnow; and the wobble like an

A wobble tackle for dead bait trolling. Note securing of hooks. On other side are further hooks. (*David Hay*)

injured fish. Both are effective, the latter especially so. Making the fish rotate on its long axis, like a Devon minnow, is the easier of the two options. All that is required is a standard sprat tackle for smaller baits and larger DIY versions for bigger baits. The proprietary brands either come with rigid plastic vanes or with articulated metal vanes which pinch together behind the skull. The latter are preferable as the bait is then more securely held on the metal pin.

Security of attachment is paramount. It is simply not enough to stick the hooks in appropriate parts of the bait and hope this will suffice to hook an attacking Ferox. It is absolutely essential to bind the trace and/or hooks to the bait with fine soft brass or copper wire. Aya Thorne, the British record holder, goes to the trouble of actually sewing the bait to the trace with a small bodkin needle. All this fuss is necessary because of the behaviour of Ferox in attacking the bait, a behaviour which can knock unbound hooks out of the bait, provide the Ferox with a 'free' meal and the angler with a bruised ego.

From bitter experience and from the writings of others it is important to consider how a Ferox goes about striking at the bait. The response of the fish is dependant on three main sensory stimuli: visual, olfactory and aural or VOA for short in other words, sight, smell and sound (more precisely vibration). Wobbled or spun fresh dead baits provide all three; lures only two. Ferox will repeatedly attack a dead bait, but will generally only attack an artificial lure once. Several authors give accounts of Ferox holding on to a natural bait, being dragged along with the boat for tens of yards only to release the bait and attack it again, sometimes more than once. This proves several things. Ferox are not frightened of boats, do not worry about the tackle and realise full well when they are on to the real thing. I have observed a Ferox grabbing my bait within a few feet of the boat after three failed attacks. It is certainly an exciting experience, but a sad one indeed to watch a whopper win the bait from your trace. It is a learning experience too, especially in the correct binding and positioning of the hooks on the bait.

I think Ferox have several attacking techniques which need to be covered by the secure attachment of the hooks and trace. The first one is, for lack of a better expression, a form of 'kung-fu' head butt. The Ferox simply acts like a toothy torpedo and slams full tilt into the fish. The power of this head butt is quite astonishing. I have had the skulls of substantial dead baits caved in as if by hammer blow. If you have not bound the hooks on properly then at the same time as the bait's cranium is crushed the hooks are thrown clear leaving the Ferox with a simple mopping up task at your expense. You can almost guarantee this if repeated attacks occur. The next attack mode of the Ferox is to have several perfunctory lunges at the bait, registered on your rod as a series of gentle pulls, followed by a seizure of your bait, usually across the middle. This I term the 'knock and grip' attack, eventually causing your rod to go round in a pulsating curve. The curve convincing as it may appear, may disappear if the Ferox has not gripped a hook in its jaws at the same time. The third main method of attack is a combination of both, in an all engulfing swoop at the bait either head on or tail first. The last form of attack is more common when small baits are used and usually results in a well-hooked fish. However, large Ferox, such as the one mentioned in the above account of the 11lb fish at Arkaig, can do this with even herring-size baits. The 'knock and grip' attack is more prevalent with big baits and the head butt can happen with either. I feel that the head butt attack is the one that produces most secondary attacks, because presumably it is something that a Ferox will do when attacking a living fish, or shoal of fish. By killing a fish or smashing into a shoal of fish 'head butt style' it can then pick up injured fish or casualties very readily.

All the likely methods of attack require a careful consideration of hook distribution on the bait, especially on large baitfish. This is every bit as important as proper binding. If you buy a proprietary sprat tackle then it will come reasonably well-armed with a fairly good hook spread relative to the fish that can be mounted on it. It may be necessary though to add to this, as some tackles leave the tail unarmed. The basic rule of a treble hook in

Blade spinner attachment, upper spinning tackle of the archer type. (*David Hay*)

head, middle and tail is a golden one, but it requires reinforcement in bigger baits by the addition of more trebles on mid-flank, on both sides of the bait. In this case you are preparing for the 'knock and grip' attack. The best solution to this for both spun and wobbled baits is to have an array of five, yes five trebles. (Do not discuss this technique loudly in a pub as it may cost you a fair amount of money if the bar staff think you are placing an order.) These five trebles should be positioned with three in the 'golden rule' position in one flank, supplemented by two mid-flank on the other. Fairly large trebles relative to the size of the bait are better than smaller ones. Ferox are not generally tackle-shy and it is wrong to assign to them a cunning intelligence they palpably do not have. For baits in the nine- to twelve-inch size range I normally use size two or one and for smaller fish down to size eight. If you are using baits that require smaller hooks than this then you are either into 'tiddler bashing' or collecting more bait!

Even if you take all the above precautions you will still lose fish. There is no way round this and it just becomes part of the uncertainty that makes our sport so worthwhile. In wild trout fishing you never know what you are going to get, let alone know that an artificially reared record was put in three days ago. The anticipation, the tales of battles won and lost, are part of the driving force to fish for Ferox. In the end the integrity of the struggle becomes a victory in itself. On two occasions, one following another through twenty-six blank trolling hours, we have had well-prepared sprat tackles attacked by substantial Ferox only to lose the fish and have the bait returned to us like a fish skeleton in a Tom and Jerry cartoon. One of the Ferox in question even forced open the articulated spinning vanes in the process. We christened this fish 'the engineer'. As far as we know it is still alive and well in Loch Rannoch, though missing two of its double-figure friends, which were our reward for relentlessly overcoming this setback.

Mounting a natural bait on a sprat tackle provides a simple and effective method of presenting a real fish to tempt a Ferox. There are however two main disadvantages. One is the limited size range of factory-made tackles available, and the other is that the vanes can act as a 'lever' for the Ferox to unhook itself, should a large fish engulf the bait head on. Even a large treble placed in the skull of the bait can be obscured by the vanes. The size problem can be overcome by some DIY activity, and both problems can be avoided by the use of a wobble tackle. A wobbled bait is to my mind the single most effective method for catching Ferox. Although a modicum of skill is required to mount the baitfish in such a way as to achieve the most enticing action and to secure a good hook hold, it is readily acquired with a little patience and experiment.

The bait depends for its wobbling action in the water, when trolled, on a bend imparted either by a soft metal pin inserted in the fish through its mouth, or the curvature caused by unevenly tensioning a trace of hooks on

A wobble tackle showing hook arrangements from above (again note wiring of hooks). (*David Hay*)

one side of the fish. The former is the more easily achieved. Old coat hangers cut up into various lengths are a useful source of pins, as are giant-sized paper clips. Lengths of twelve gauge fence wire are another alternative. The main thing is to choose a length of pin that will go through to the very stem of the tail ('caudal peduncle' in scientific parlance). You can either pre-bend the pin before insertion or, with tough or slightly frozen fish, bend the fish after the pin is inserted. The correct degree of bend takes a wee bit of trial and error to achieve the broad, sweeping, slow turning arc that looks irresistible. If you are any kind of instinctive angler, you will know the bend is right when you see it. Personally I prefer the bend to be concentrated on the last two thirds of the bait. Ferox are not conversant with geometry so there is no need to develop a complex. Experience is your best guide. Get some in, for working out the wobble can win you a whopper.

The alternative method of bending the baitfish is by threading your line through the fish and then tying on your hook trace and pulling back. You then embed the hooks in a requisite position to adhere to the 'golden rule' and maintain the bend in the fish. There is a wee bit of a knack in this, but it does not take long to master. The best method is to thread, by use of a large needle or bait pin, in through the mouth of the bait-fish and out through the back of the skull. If you use a long shaft salmon double fly hook you can pull this back through into the mouth of the fish and attach to the main line. This long shaft hook also be used for the attachment of a blade spinner as an

Assorted weight and attractor items. (*David Hay*)

added attraction. I used to thread the line through the mouth and out the vent. This achieved an excellent bend, but transgressed the golden rule and frequently Ferox would get some free water ski-ing lessons whilst escaping with half the bait.

Some people simple achieve the wobble by the effect of the hook trace itself. Placing a large single hook through both jaws of the bait then bending the fish with the placement of the rest of the hook trace. This is something I try to avoid. Ideally the baitfish, on the occasion of a firm strike from a Ferox, should run up the line in the manner of a Devon minnow, leaving only the business end in the jaws of the quarry. I always start looking for fresh underwear when I see the whole fish clamped in a Ferox's jaw as it nears the boat, as it often means the chance of an insecure hook hold. The thread-through method obviates this horrible fear, and by threading through a hoop in the pin rather than attaching the hook trace directly to it the same can apply to the pin method. Another way to achieve this is simply to add a pin loose in the body of the fish after thread-through. Some diagrams and illustrations are provided of trace set-ups on pages 82, 84, 85. Clamping the jaws of the baitfish helps to achieve a better wobble, and some authors recommend cutting off the fins. I have never found this necessary except with the dorsal fin of a male grayling.

These then are the basics of using a natural bait. There are many variations and modifications. Trolling is a major sub-culture in the states of the Pacific coast of Canada and the USA. If you wish to get into a more technological approach then it is well worth reading books and magazines from this part of the world. Some of them appear to go 'over the top' in terms of the ordinary pleasure angler in this country, but some modified ideas are worth considering. Rod stacking systems and outrigger booms that allow a multitude of lines to be used at the same time are to my mind more hassle than they are worth and, in any case, might transgress sporting rules here. Not so with in-line attractors such as mentioned earlier, though these are a far cry from the aquatic 'coal scuttles' used in attracting Pacific salmon.

So far I have not said too much about rod, reels and line. Line is the most important of the three and, in addition to the lines mentioned above, lead core and metal lines can be used very effectively. They are not essential and you can succeed without them, but they always add another string to the bow, if you will excuse the pun. Trolling tube flies and tandem lures is successful in catching Ferox, and nothing more is needed than normal salmon tackle and a selection of 'dead budgies' masquerading as panto-mime flies.

We are now able to choose from a range of rods undreamt of by our angling ancestors. These rods, and especially the materials they are made from, render any comments of the crudity of Ferox trolling redundant. Pike and carp rods with a test curve of 1½-2½ lb will cover most needs. Salmon spinning and worming rods are my favourite choice because of the short handles which make their positioning in the rod-holders in the boat more comfortable for the user. Carp and pike rods these days tend to have long handles which protrude into the leg room area of the boat. In lochs where I know the Ferox seldom exceed 10lb, I sometimes use a general purpose float rod. This is a real sporting approach but this type of rod is not suitable for trolling large dead baits. Most beginners make the mistake of thinking that short rods are the order of the day for boat work. This is not the case in trolling. What is required are rods in the order of ten to fourteen feet in length. These, when mounted on gunwale rod-holders, maximise the distance between the trolling lines and make line crossing, when turning the boat, much less likely. Once you have crossed lines for the first time you will wish the rods were a mile long. It is quite simply a way of making the Gordian knot look like something a kitten might play with.

Reels for Ferox fishing should also come from the wide range of salmon, carp and pike reels on the market. Again it is not worth being too fussy about this. Fixed spool, multipliers and centrepin can all be used satisfactorily. My personal preference is for a fixed spool reel from the carp or pike range, which has a free spool function and a high gear ratio. In the Ferox-85 Group we still have on-board debates about the relative merits of multipliers. Some of us swear by them, others at them. They certainly proved their worth in the capture of a record trout. Centrepin and large fly reels also have their devotees, and the direct contact with a fighting fish they offer is certainly appealing. The main thing is to have a reel you can depend on. Just because you will not be casting and retrieving a lot does not mean to say that you can ignore the requirements of the reel to wind in heavy dead baits or for fighting a powerful fish. Regrettably some anglers still seem to think, 'Oh well, it's only for trolling, I can use any old rubbish'. Rather them than me.

Now that the requisite main and terminal tackle has been selected, the baits and lures chosen, and the protective clothing suitable for a ten-hour sub-Arctic session has been donned, some consideration of the boat arrangement and trolling procedure is now due. Apart from your brain the most important part of your anatomy in trolling is your backside. (From what I have seen of the approach that some anglers have to Ferox fishing, this body part seems to do more of the thinking than the cranium.) Padded seats or a cushion can increase your durability and let you hang on long enough to catch a fish. A portable latrine is useful too. No point in frequent visits ashore. You will not find many Ferox there.

Rod-holders are vital. Mounted on the gunwales they leave your hands free for more pleasant tasks, apart from the physical benefits in more trouble-free trolling. If you are not experienced in trolling then two side-mounted rods are enough to start with. Later, as you gain experience, a stern-mounted rod can be added. Some people use a stacking system and side outrigger booms to allow them to fish more rods, but I do not feel that the extra hassle is really worth it. Unless you choose a venue where there is a good professional set-up, you will probably find that rod-holders are not supplied. The best recourse is to buy a set of detachable mounts that screw, fly-tying vice style, on the gunwales. These are a far cry from being ideal and the primary option should be rod-holders that have a permanent bracket mount. This is fine if you possess a boat of your own which you can customise to your heart's content, but a boat hirer may have a 'hairy fit' if he sees you bringing out a drill and screwdriver. There are also rod-holders which mount in the rowlock mounting holes. These are fine if your engine does not break down and you have time to remove them before smashing onto the rocks. It is worth going to a wee bit of bother over the basic rod mounting preparation, as holding rods all day or botching up some temporary fixture detracts from both enjoyment and efficiency. Again, if you wish to take a more high technology approach then the American catalogues will take you into a highly absorbing and expensive world of wonder. While you are doing that I will have put some more rod hours in. Technology is no substitute for relentlessness and it is much more damaging to your wallet.

Echo sounders are useful especially with down riggers but do not guarantee success.

This applies especially to echo-sounders and downriggers. I never cease to be amused by the glee with which newcomers to Ferox angling react to these items of technology. Charged up with enthusiasm after reading the catalogue propaganda they innocently assume that they are going to track down an individual Ferox at a known depth, troll a bait past its nose at the requisite depth and hook it forthwith. Well, the looks of disappointment on their faces are interesting even if the results are not. An angler can approach a shoal of rising fish in a river, cast his fly at a chosen individual fish, in top style, and still not catch it. Why does anyone think a Ferox is going to be any more obliging?

There is no real point in getting a downrigger without an echo-sounder (unless you are a very skilful map reader) and preferably one with a depth alarm buzzer. This will let you set a warning depth slightly more than your selected depth, and allow you to adjust your position to deeper water before a foul-up occurs. Some space age downriggers come with an automatic sonar and electric motor winch system, which adjusts to a preset distance from the bottom. Both echo-sounders and downriggers have their place in the approach, but over reliance on them is not advisable. Echo-sounders to some extent replace the knowledge of the old ghillies as do outboards their muscle power. St John, in his book *Wild Sports of the Highlands*, gives the advice, 'A patient fisherman should find out how deep every reach and bay of the lake is before he begins to troll. The labour of the day spent in taking soundings is well repaid.' In the sense that they will increase your knowledge of the water you are fishing in, echo-sounders are very worthwhile indeed and can save from the efforts of the last century. It is possible to catch fish on a day when little is showing on the screen, and also to have a day when the machine shows massive numbers of fish, yet none are caught. Treat with mild scepticism the size of the fish indicated by the electronic icons on the screen. Even very expensive echo-sounders employed by fisheries research institutes will not tell you whether a fish is just below or just above a record size, so do not read too much into the screen images. No echo-sounder that I am aware of can tell you what species of fish its ping is bouncing off. Is that big icon indicating a fish at ninety feet just off the bottom a huge Ferox or a large eel 'tail walking'? You do not know for certain and this is part of the fun of it all. Remember too all those decades, indeed centuries, of angling for Ferox that went on without the benefit of these technological advances and yet produced so many memorable fish. So if your budget does not stretch to sophisticated silicon chip wizardry you can rest assured this will not prevent you from catching your quarry.

So, simple or sophisticated you are now ready to venture forth to your chosen venue. Honed to a fine sense of anticipation, what are your chances? Cheerfully, the best odds I can give you are three to one against. You might be the lucky tyro who hits one in the first half hour. A famous TV

Trolling into the gloaming often brings results. Note long rods to give maximum distance between lines.

personality we took out once caught a Ferox of 7½lb exactly twenty-one minutes into her first outing (there were some jealous male anglers at BBC headquarters apparently, so we did not get a free licence that year). Depend on your relentlessness more than good fortune. The chances are you are going to blank. I once went twelve straight outings averaging nine hours per outing, without catching a single thing; on the thirteenth outing I caught a 12lb Ferox. It was nothing to do with tackle, skill or bait. Several times our group members have experienced several blank days only to have three hits in the space of an hour in the next session. Others, who gave up and went flyfishing, missed out on an experience that changed our angling lives. Stick with it, for remember what you are up against. Loch Ness for example has a greater volume of fresh water in it than the combined total of all waters in England and Wales. You are trying to locate a fish three feet long which can move in three different directions. You are moving too. If you were working out the odds of hitting inanimate objects this size with your lure what chances would you give yourself? The only positive feature is that there are probably more Ferox than you think and some at least will be actively seeking food. Basically what you are attempting to do is to place your bait or lure within sufficient distance of a hungry Ferox. The fish has the final choice not you. Ferox are not likely to be hungry for very long or they would not reach the sizes and growth rates that they do achieve. Keep at it until you find a hungry one and remember another quotation from St John: 'You may pass over the heads of hundreds of large trout when they are lying at rest and not hungry, and you will not catch one; but as soon as they begin to feed, a fish, although he may have half-a-dozen small trout in his stomach, will still run at your bait.'

A fine ferox double (12½ and 16lb) taken in an hour after three consecutive blank days. Relentless ness has rewards!

This difficulty in catching any number of Ferox is long known. A quotation of Cholmondeley Pennell given by the Reverend Houghton in 1879 says: 'As a rule however, not much success attends the troller for the Great Lake Trout – a circumstance which may possibly be in some measure attributable to the general ignorance of all its habits, and the manner in which it is to be fished for.' So if you blank you can take comfort from your adherence to a well-established tradition and renew your determination for the next time. The scarcity of Ferox in anglers' catches is also known to modern science. Dr Niall Campbell in his scientific paper in the 1979 issue of the *Journal of Fisheries Biology* says: 'Although it is probable that upwards of a million brown trout are caught each season by Scotland's estimated 75,000 to 100,000 anglers, usually less than five notable Ferox a year are reported in the press or represented by scales sent to the Freshwater Fisheries Laboratory.' This statement was one of the motivating factors in the formation of the Ferox-85 Group, and while probably more Ferox are caught than supposed, by these criteria it hardly points to Ferox being a major feature of the national trout catch.

These statements above are not meant to put you off Ferox fishing for life. They are there to give you a true insight into the difficulties which await you. Ferox angling is about quality not quantity. In these days of put-and-take fisheries some anglers seem to have lost the appetite for the total appreciation of the outdoor experience. Ferox fishing might not be for you if your expectations are fulfilled by fishing in what amounts in my opinion to a large bathtub full of finless wonder stockies. Learn to appreciate the totality of the 'Ferox experience' and you will never regret, at least in retrospect, those days when you returned fishless. The best place to observe a loch is on it. The wildlife, scenery, weather and, most important of all, the company of good friends can make any day memorable. Remember the old adage 'a bad day's fishing is better than a good day at work'! So much for the Protestant work ethic of my forebears.

Now it's not all gloom and doom of course. There are those wonderful glory days of multiple catches or the capture of an especially large individual fish. These days intersperse with those which a famous football commentator once described, after watching a particularly poor, goalless local derby on a sleety November day, as 'Nothing, nothing and nothing!' History and modern experience indicate that these glory days are well worth the effort spent with no great success. Osgood Mackenzie, in his book *A Hundred Years in the Highlands*, gives the catch of 12 April 1851 taken by Sir Alexander Gordon-Cumming in the Fionn Loch as comprising twelve trout weighing a total of eighty-seven pounds twelve ounces. This included five fish between 10 and 14lb and two over 5lb; a remarkable day's fishing by any standards. In 1849, Major Cheape took twenty-five Ferox in a single season from Loch Rannoch, and followed this notable achievement with the memorable capture of a 21lb fish in 1867. These magnificent catches are not just a feature of the past. In the 1989 and 1990 seasons alone the Ferox-85 group caught fifty fish over 5lb including a string of notable doubles. One of the lochs we fished produced over twenty Ferox in a single season and of course Loch Awe produced a new record in 1993. The Ferox are still there. All it takes is serious preparation, a sense of self-deprecatory humour and that favourite word of mine – relentlessness.

All this of course will come to no avail if your 'on water' approach is not considered. Long gone are the days of the Highland ghillie well-versed in the nuances of approach taken on his local patch. This kind of knowledge is still available to some extent in Ireland, but for the most part has been lost elsewhere in the British Isles, and therefore you will be faced with a mission of rediscovery. Just place it on your schedule of the total Ferox experience. You will probably, in the process, learn a lot more about yourself too.

Luckily we can still draw on the experience of the past thanks to some of

The end of an eight year angling odyssey – the British record trout 'safe' in our hands!

the distinguished 'ancient sages' mentioned above. We can also weld this to more modern experience and hopefully take it further as the seasons of our own experience progress. St John thought that there were three basic ingredients to success in Ferox fishing: 'Choose the roughest wind that your boat can live in; fish with a good-sized bait, not much less than a herring; and do not commence your trolling until two o'clock in the afternoon, by which time the large fish seem to have digested their last night's supper and to be again on the move.' The first two rules have been covered to some extent earlier in the chapter. The size of the bait concurs with my own personal experience and others' in the Ferox-85 Group. Perhaps Mr St John was turning a necessity into a virtue regarding the roughness of conditions. Rough weather frequently occurs in the Ferox environment and you just have to make the best of it. Certainly we have had some bumper catches during some very windy weather, of pike as well as Ferox. If you have the right boat you can take advantage; if not, you will most probably regret not taking the advice offered earlier. I think the importance of weather conditions are exaggerated. My personal preference is for a moderate north-west breeze of polar maritime air mass, with just the beginnings of whitecaps on the water. My least favourite conditions are calm thundery weather, which certainly suits the midges very well, if not the Ferox. We have caught Ferox in most weather conditions safe enough to launch a boat, and also have blanked in what appears to be perfect

The faces of the Ferox 85 'special relentless squadron' say it all. The heroes' happy return.

conditions. There is no substitute for relentless effort, so do not resort to the old excuse of conditions not being amenable if the real cause of your failure was an early procrastinating visit to the pub. Perseverance may prevent you from becoming just another useless 'plonker' who talks a good game but can't play. There are no coffee-table catches in Ferox fishing.

The advice on timing offered by St John is slightly at variance with the recommendation of Cholmondeley Pennell, again quoted by the Reverend Houghton: 'As a rule, *begin* fishing when other people are *leaving off* – that is, about six o'clock pm. Up to this hour the fish are rarely in a position from which they can by any accident see your bait. From six o'clock until midnight lake trout may be caught. These fish are essentially night feeders. During the day they lie hid under rocks and in holes, in the deepest part of the extensive lakes which they generally inhabit, and only venture into fishable water at the approach of evening.'

From my own experiences and that of friends it is obvious that there are indeed peak times of the day for catching Ferox, though if you asked me the best times to start Ferox fishing my immediate suggestion would be to say from dawn on 15 March until dusk on 6 of October. If you are not on the water you cannot catch fish. From our experiences the peak time for catches varies seasonally. In March and April we generally reckon the best time to be between mid-day and three in the afternoon. Gradually this gets later during the day as the year progresses, until by mid-summer we sometimes do not commence fishing until mid-evening. Catching a Ferox in the afterglow of a West Highland sunset on a still June evening is one of the most moving of all angling experiences. Unless of course you have forgotten the midge repellent; then you are moved in a different manner. Towards the end of August the cycle reverses again and, by September, mid-afternoon or early evening becomes the favoured time. This is only a broad generalisation and it is possible to catch good Ferox at other times of day. The peak times also vary a little depending on the venue. Experience is the mother of progress once more. Our experience in judging the best months of the year for Ferox concurs closely with that of Sir John Colqhoun, who wrote last century: 'The best time of year for *Salmo ferox* is the end of April, May and the beginning of June. They are very dormant all July and August, particularly if the weather be hot. Although much more shy than in spring, they sometimes take pretty fair in September.' May is the most treacherous month for weather in northern Britain, and remember the old adage about casting cloots too early. The first week in particular is noted for an outbreak of Arctic air which brings blizzards that will make you a 'casting clot' if you have abandoned your thermal protection too soon.

A further three major recommendations were outlined by Cholmondeley Pennell. These concerned depth, speed and place. His comments on depth were: 'Instead of weighing your tackle to spin at from three to four feet from the *surface*, lead it so to sink within about the same distance from the *bottom*, be the depth what it may.' Much the same opinion was held by Sir John Colqhoun: 'The truth is, when trolling for the *Salmo ferox*, the baits should be hung only a few yards from the bottom. They must therefore frequently catch a weed, or root or sunk rock. Be assured that the largest fish are generally taken by trolling close to the bottom, as they are lazy.' Our own more recent trolling adventures largely back the veracity of the above advice. Being bottom-oriented is a good starting off point, but again prepared be to be flexible.

Newcomers to trolling or the uninitiated quoting other poorly informed sources frequently assume that Ferox always inhabit the great depths of a loch. This is not the case at all. Ferox of course do go down to great depths, but they are not permanent residents there. In April we often catch Ferox only a few yards from the shore in less than thirty feet of water. On the other hand, at various times of the year, we have caught Ferox near the bottom at one hundred feet, at the surface over the deepest parts and in mid-water at eighty feet over three hundred feet of water.

Judging the depth to fish and then achieving consistency is one of the most important features of Ferox fishing. It is not always easy to achieve, and the nagging doubt that you are never quite where you want to be

Some Ferox do not spawn every year and can remain in good condition even in winter as this photograph taken in February indicates. *(A. F. Walker)*

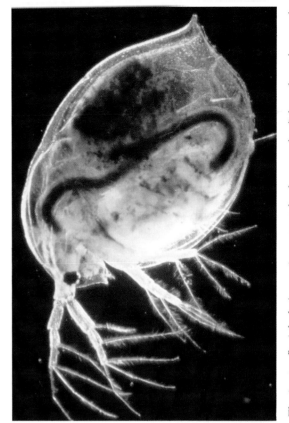

The 'water flea' *daphnia* – an important food source for fish such as charr and powan. *(David Hay)*

Loch Bhrodain charr in all their autumnal glory. *(A. F. Walker)*

Pea mussels are an important food source for charr in Highland lochs. *(David Hay)*

Top: Tagging trials have given valuable insights of the biology of Ferox in Scandinavia. Such trials have not been carried out to any great extent in Britain.

Bottom: Ferox ugly? A fine 24lb hen fish destined for release after stripping of eggs for research purposes. The first Norwegian trout seen by the author.

Top: Two forms of charr from Loch Rannoch. *(Above)*, benthic, *(below)* pelagic.

Bottom: The white spotted charr of Japan. *(Fred Kircheis)*

Top: Charr from Floods Pond, Maine, USA. *(Fred Kircheis)*

Bottom: Recently deglaciated land in Alaska – much of Britain looked like this at the end of the last Ice Age. Charr were among the first colonising animals. *(Sandy Milner)*

To begin with glacial meltwater rivers are 'milky' and have low biological diversity. Colonising charr have a hard time at first.

The Boreal Forest is excellent habitat for trout, salmon and charr although largely coniferous in nature its leaf tree species ensure food and shelter for fish. Very different indeed to monocultural plantations. (Sandy Milner)

Loch Garry (Perthshire). Typical of hydro-electric reservoirs in the Scottish Highlands – a fine home for charr and Ferox.

Eventually a more diverse ecosystem develops. This forest river in Alaska is home to several salmon species. Charr are no longer river residents in Britain. Note that the conifers are well back from the river edge and the deciduous tree fringe. (Sandy Milner)

Top:　Rapala lures are the most significant improvement in terminal tackle for Ferox in 200 years. *(David Hay)*

Bottom:　A well-conditioned Ferox of 18lb 2oz taken in March from Loch Awe by Mr Brent Gibbon of Edinburgh.

Top: A Ferox in finest fettle dispels the myth of large-headed ugliness.

Bottom: Charr learn to live under fish farm cages and gorge themselves on 'waste' food. Unfortunately this has potential ecological problems for the loch and produces podgy, ugly fish!

Top: The British record (19lb 10⅜oz) with the anti-kink and type of bait that accounted for it. It lies against a three-foot rule.

Bottom: Alistair Thorne of the Ferox 85 Group with the trout of his and everyone else's dreams.

always seems to remain with you. To judge the depth you are fishing at to any accuracy, depends on your speed, which I will comment on later. The best approach to begin with is the simplest one of using different sized lead weights. This is much more important than the length of line trolled behind the boat. Generally we work on the rule of thumb that each ounce of lead, with our boat going as slowly as the engine will go, and about thirty yards of line out, will let us achieve fifteen to twenty feet of depth in calm conditions. We calibrate this according to our sonar readings or by use of an OS map or Admiralty chart. Hitting the bottom at known depths confirms our lead loading. The actual result varies according to several factors. Of these the choice of heading into the wind or going with it, the size/type of the bait/lure used and the amount of physical or human ballast in the boat are of prime importance. There is a bit of an art in all this, which in the end you just have to develop the hard way. Once you have mastered it, the use of expensive high-tech equipment is made much less necessary. Some people deride the use of weights as detracting from the fight of the fish. This is to my mind sheer and utter humbug. A three-ounce weight is of little consequence to a 5lb Ferox, let alone a fish three times that weight. Such negative comments are usually derived either from an in-built bigotry against any form of angling which does not use a flyrod, or from pure simple jealousy. Flyfishermen, deep down, are very resentful of those who would use their day's catch as bait.

The next simplest method for achieving a preset depth, especially in very deep water, is by using a diving vane, variously called in the American literature as the 'Deep Six' or 'Dipsy Diver'. These are either disc- or shield-shaped plates with an offset weight which makes the device act like a giant version of the lip vane of a plug or Rapala. They come in a range of sizes that can let you fish at depths up to 200 feet. They operate with an adjustable tripping mechanism which frees the plate from its steep diving angle, when a strike occurs, or when it hits the bottom. The resistance is then relieved, and you can then fight a fish with minimal drag or retrieve the plate for resetting. When in operation they cause the rod to go round in a stiff bend which some people find off-putting, even alarming. When a fish hits, the rod will at first straighten and then go round in the usual way. It is a bit weird at first, but it certainly works well and the Ferox are not in the least worried about it. The diving vane is best used with the heavier test curve rods. I would not recommend its use for some prized split-cane rod or light spinning rod.

Downriggers, without a doubt, offer one of the best ways of regulating your depth of fishing with a high degree of accuracy. They also offer the chance of having nothing in the way between the fish and yourself except an anti-kink device. Proprietary brands range in price from a few tens of pounds to several hundred, depending on the degree of sophistication. The top electronically operated models come with an in-built sonar capacity linked to a winch which automatically maintains a pre-set depth. The winch on such models also offers a push-button automatic retrieval facility that winds in the lead ball after a fish has struck. Simpler models require some elbow grease. I would suggest, especially if you fish alone, that you only try one downrigger in your set-up or, simply do not use one at all. If you are trying simultaneously to fight a fish, wind in a downrigger cable, steer the boat off rocks in a gale, find the oars because the outboard has just broken down, and wind in your other lines, you may feel you should be given an Oscar for your impersonation of Basil Fawlty or Laurel and Hardy. Keep it simple or fish in a group and allot tasks to the 'crew'. Downriggers can be extremely useful items, but remember with every big step forward comes a little step backwards.

There is a huge difference between speed and haste as we are often told. In Ferox fishing there is little room for the former and no place at all for the latter. Speed concerned our predecessors greatly and I wonder how much the ghillies of previous centuries might have appreciated an outboard on the long rows down the lochs. Rowing still is an excellent way of trolling a bait or lure. We cannot expect these days to employ a youth and an old man with a withered arm to row twenty miles a day as Sir John Colqhoun did, and I think that after a few hours of this form of propulsion you will be glad of the modern two-stroke or four-stroke 'ghillie' (unless of course it is my detested fiend the 'Seagull'). The ideal situation, if you can afford it, is to have a big powerful engine for rapid transit between likely 'hot spots' and a small, low horsepower trolling motor for fishing. Even outboards of fifteen horsepower can operate at suitably low speeds. If in doubt, an adjustable 'trolling plate' can be fitted near the propeller to reduce speed when required. Ferox do not appear to be concerned with the noise of the outboard. Electric motors are not strictly necessary, though four-stroke are more pleasurable for use than two-stroke engines and represent the biggest improvement in outboards since Seagulls were consigned to the scrapheap.

Most of the advice given by nineteenth-century experts advocated slow movement. Cholmondeley Pennell's comments on speed were: 'Let your boat be rowed *slowly*, rather than at a brisk lively pace, as a large lake trout will seldom trouble himself to follow a bait that is moving fast away from him; consequently your bait must possess the speciality of spinning at all events moderately well or it will not spin at all.' Sir John Colqhoun proffers: 'In roughish weather row slowly in order to give them a good opportunity of seeing and seizing the bait; quicker in a mild clear day, for it is then as well to give them little time to reflect.' The latter advice fits more closely with our experiences since 1985. Ferox will take a bait presented at various speeds, and though to go too slowly is probably a lot better than going too fast, it is not always the slowest speed which gains more strikes. We have captured several large Ferox whilst we had a stiff wind at our stern which moved us well beyond the slowest speed possible. Bruce Macauslan generally preferred a brisk walking pace for trolling and seldom went as slowly as the boat was capable of.

Perhaps the most important advice in the pursuit of Ferox concerns their location. Echo-sounders are not as much help as they might at first appear to be, though they are extremely useful in determining the physical features which make for a good Ferox 'mark'. Implicit in this statement is a conviction that Ferox are not randomly distributed within a lake. There are definite hot spots within a water body that consistently produce fish and others which seldom come up with the 'goods'. Again the 'ancient wisdom of the sages' is there to guide us. Pennell and St John provide us with some tips. The former suggests: 'The place to spin over is where the bank shelves rapidly into deep water, say at a depth of from fifteen to thirty or forty feet, according to the nature of the basin; a much greater or much less depth is useless. This is rather an important point, as thereupon it depends whether your bait is ever seen by the fish you wish to catch. The food of the lake trout consists of small fish. These are not to be found in any great depths of water, but on the contrary on the sloping shores of the lake, up which, therefore, the trout comes in search of them, stopping short of the shallows.' There is much in this advice that is very sound indeed. The Ferox has two choices in finding its food: it can lie in wait like a lion at a waterhole in ambush of its prey; or it can go and actively pursue them like a cheetah on the plain. Both approaches are sometimes taken. I think the first approach is largely responsible for known hot spots, especially during the spring descent of salmon smolts, and the second accounts for the presence of Ferox in open mid-water. I have occasionally observed, during calm weather, Ferox slamming into charr shoals near the surface, with the charr leaping out of the water to evade capture.

Finding these marks or hot spots takes a lot of time and effort. I am of course not going to impart my own hard-won knowledge of any particular loch, but I will say that if you catch a Ferox in one spot then concentrate some time there, rather than become a tourist. The extremities of the loch and any major geographical features are worth extra effort. Sir John Colqhoun gives sound advice which our own experience vindicates: 'In the early part of the season the points keep most fish. As the year advances, the bays are the surest find. In autumn a heavy fish is often hooked about the mouths or estuaries of rivers or burns, which earlier in the season would have been trolled in vain.' This advice is sound indeed, but I would also remind you that during the smolt run the mouths of salmon streams are worth some attention. I once caught a trout of 2lb, in a favoured site for trout ambushing smolts, that contained eight salmon smolts. Trout can gorge themselves at this time and in a feeding frenzy are easily fooled into taking a lure. In identifying likely 'marks' remember that favoured spots may change according not only to the season, but to the time of day, the weather and the level of the loch. This last is especially true of hydro-electric reservoirs, an environment that Ferox 'sages' did not have great experience of 150 years ago. In learning you can only travel well in Ferox fishing and you never seem to arrive, but the journey is worth it. This is no more true than in finding out the favoured haunts of our adversary.

The general approach we take to presenting our baits or lures is to fish with three rods with baits of different sizes and different weighting or depth setting. We also put different lengths of line out. There is no great need for distances behind the boat of more than thirty to fifty yards. The diversity of this procedure is aimed both at locating Ferox and avoiding line crosses and tangles. We play a team game with three members: one person on the outboard; another in charge of the technical side; and another on galley duty. Normally we start off with lures and the 'technician' mounts the real baits whilst we are on the water ready for action. Not a moment is wasted in this way. The heaviest leaded bait is put on the outside rod and the shortest line is fished from the stern mounting.

Unless we are at a new venue we start right away at known marks. We tend to follow the shore contours avoiding known snags. In this the echo-sounder is of great value. Gentle turns of the boat are in order, and if a sharp turn is required the stern line is brought in. Contrary to some advice given we have not found it necessary to keep the boat on the turn. If a fish strikes the procedure is quickly to retrieve the other two lines and/or downrigger line. The understandable instinct of beginners is generally first to pick up the rod with the fish. This is a serious mistake, however tempting it may be. Have some patience; after ten hours, what is a few moments more?

To begin with it is difficult to determine what is a fish strike and what is merely a bump on the bottom. Fairly quickly you learn the difference not only between these, but also simply from the curve and action of the rod what size of fish has attacked. It is amazing that no matter how weary you are, as soon as a fish hits you are wide awake with the adrenalin flowing in your veins. When a fish hit is identified it is a good idea to rev up the engine to help sink the hooks. The procedure for fighting the fish varies a little according to whether you are going with the wind or against. The ideal position is to get downwind of and broadside on to the fish, so that you are not drifting on top of it. Have no doubts that if the fish has half a chance it will go under the boat. Teamwork is important here. On a calm day it is enough to put the engine into neutral and fight from there. However, on a stormy or choppy day careful repositioning is necessary to maintain the fighting position. Whatever you do, try to avoid beaching the boat and fighting from the shore. The ideal is to fight the Ferox over deep water with as much distance between the rocky and snaggy shores and your dream fish as possible. Alistair Thorne once lost a huge trout in Rannoch that snagged the line on rocks as it headed towards shore, and I had similar experience with a pike on Laggan.

Things are more difficult if you hook a fish when going into a stiff wind. The procedure here is gradually and slowly to head out at a shallow angle, eventually swinging round so that you get downwind of the fish. It is quite a nerve-racking experience at first, especially if you do not have an adequate boat.

Regardless of direction, most often the initial reaction of the fish is almost one of surprise. The fish comes in, without too much trouble, for the first few yards and the tyro may believe the fight is over and the pub yarns he was told about past battles are myths. The fight is just beginning, however, and as soon as the fish comes within a few rod lengths of the boat you know there has been no exaggeration. Aya Thorne fought the record trout for twenty minutes before it broke surface and took a further fifteen minutes to land it. It is not a good idea to try to net the fish too early, though it may be tempting because the fight is so close to the boat. More side strain is needed than on a shore-based fight, because the fish frequently tries to head for the bow or stern. Whatever you do don't let it get anywhere near the engine. On only two occasions have we had the pleasure of two takes at the same time. Some quick thinking is necessary in this situation. If you cannot judge the size of the fish immediately then deal with the one that took the biggest bait first. Get the other fishless rod out of the way and let battle begin. As soon as you have ascertained the bigger of the two then deal with this first in the usual manner. The smaller fish should be kept at bay until the bigger is landed. Landing the Ferox requires a salmon-sized landing net with big mesh. Knotless micro-mesh nets are a nightmare when it comes to removing a multiple treble hook tackle or plug. Gaffs, like Seagull engines, belong perhaps to the palaeolithic dreamtime.

OK, you have now followed all procedures and your relentlessness has been rewarded with a trout that most people just dream about. What then do you do about it? Well as a native Caledonian I consider myself as entitled as an Inuit or Sami to dine upon my native faunal resources. Make no mistake about it: Ferox make a fine meal. They have, when in good condition, a bright red flesh as tasty as a good salmon or sea trout. Negative comments on their taste and texture probably derive from fish in poor condition and the usual anti-Ferox mythology, based on ignorance. Perhaps you will consider a glass case a better destination than the fish-kettle, and certainly a wild trout over 10lb is a worthy subject.

The other option is to release the fish to fight another day. I am by profession and inclination a conservationist. I am however not one who panders to the sentimentalities of the coffee-table, eco-panic sub-culture of

No need to kill every fish. Small Ferox especially should be spared for better times to come.

recent years. Fish are like people in the sense that they cannot die twice. It does not matter to an individual fish how it dies, whether by hook, tooth, spear or claw; total disruption of its central nervous system occurs. Osprey, otter or angler, the fish does not make a value judgement. We of course can and there is no point in killing for killing's sake. So if it is lightly hooked, and even on multiple hook tackles this is possible, and if you have no use for the fish, then let it go. It actually in some ways makes better sense to let the smaller Ferox go. Old large fish are more likely to have spawned and left their genetic inheritance for the future. They are going to die shortly anyway. Young Ferox are the dreams of your own tomorrow. Part of the ethos of the Ferox-85 Group is to collect scientific data, and we retain fish for certain forms of analysis. Even released fish can provide information, especially with regard to scale samples which can be taken without undue harm to the fish. You can help in this process and have good sport at the same time.

Many of you reading this book will not be in the fortunate financial position of being able to buy your own boat and equipment or to hire these on a frequent basis. Do not be dismayed. I was not myself born with a silver spoon in my mouth, and even if I had been I would have made a spinner for Ferox out of it. For many years my Ferox fishing was from the bank with fairly standard pike tackle. Ferox can be readily caught from the bank. It is even more important in this situation to know of particular places to concentrate on. River inlets and outlets are good starting points, as are inlets and outlets of hydro-electric tunnels. Points and bays with sharp drop-offs are also worth concentrating some effort on.

Standard spinning techniques are efficient, but may conflict with salmon fishing interests. This is less of a problem in hydro-electric lochs which have lost their salmon run. Worming, live baiting and dead baiting are less contentious options in this context, though live baiting has come into disfavour in recent years. If morally unacceptable to you, this still leaves plenty of other options.

Worming for Ferox can produce very good results. I have seen Ferox of up to 9lb taken this way, and rumour has it that a 20lb fish was taken from Rannoch in this manner. The most favoured method is a bunch of large lobworms mounted either on a ledger or paternoster tackle. I prefer the latter method. Instead of merely a lead at the bottom of the paternoster I add a lump of Plasticene moulded into a ball. When cast in, instead of leaving it static in the usual bovine manner of setline fishers, I bounce and twitch the bait in a slow retrieve. The Plasticene breaks off if caught on the bottom and saves loss of tackle. This method, scaled down in size and using a fly cast loaded with maggots, is also very useful for catching charr.

Much the same approach can be taken using small fish as bait either live or dead. A spun or wobbled dead bait fished 'drop minnow' style is a popular technique in Highland lochs. I know of two Ferox of over 17lb taken this way. And at the fishery run by the Loch Garry Tree Group in Perthshire, I had the pleasure of informing a group of unsuccessful anglers, who claimed that the loch was fishless, that two teenage brothers had just caught Ferox of 7 and 10¾lb on the drop minnow.

That Ferox take a moving dead bait is common knowledge in angling. What comes as a surprise to many who fish for trout is that they will also take a static dead bait, fished in the way that one would normally use for pike or eels. Pike anglers who frequently fish in upland lochs are probably more aware of this than the normal trout angler. The only problem for the would-be Ferox angler in lochs also containing pike is that the pike will often get to his dead bait first. This is not the case in many Highland lochs, which have no native pike stocks.

The propensity for Ferox taking static dead baits was, however, well-known in the past. Osgood Mackenzie in *A Hundred Years in the Highlands* writes: 'As there were no boats on the loch, the old crofter population, who lived around its shores in their sheiling bothies, used to catch fish by tying a cod-hook to the end of a long string, baiting it with a good-sized trout and throwing it as far as possible out into the loch from certain points and promontories best known to themselves.' Later in the same chapter he goes on to mention the success of lines baited with parr; set overnight, they were responsible for the capture of two Ferox of twelve pounds.

That the 'noble' Ferox was not averse to a wee bit of opportunistic scavenging was also commented upon by W.C.G. St John in his book *Wild Sports of the Highlands*: 'The trout seldom take a dead bait during the daytime, but we often caught them on hooks left in the water all night.' When I first heard from my colleague Dr Niall Campbell about Osgood Mackenzie's use of the dead bait in the Fionn Loch and read of these late comments of St John, I must admit to a bit of scepticism. Until I tried it out myself. Logically of course it makes sense. In eating a dead fish a Ferox expends minimum energy for maximum gain. Overnight fishing also makes sense too, for then smell rather than sight may be the main sensory stimulation in finding food.

In making use of dead baits I also drew on my years of experience in netting charr for research purposes. It was a common experience for myself and other researchers that in those lochs which contained eels, these fish

A 12lb ferox taken at dusk after eight blank hours.

preferred to attack and eat charr caught in the gill-nets rather than the trout. This was such a severe problem at times that entire samples of charr were lost. There was obviously something about charr that was especially attractive to eels. If this was true for one species of fish then why not another? Another thing struck me too. When I was processing charr to obtain scientific data I noticed that charr left a distinctive smell on my fingers that was very difficult to get rid of. Taking these points together I decided to put theory into practice. The results were astounding.

Fishing using dead baits, ledgered or paternostered, in Loch Garry (Perthshire) in the first year produced an eighty per cent success rate, provided of course we used dead charr. Trout, sprats and even that close relative of Arctic charr, Brook charr (*Salvelinus fontinalis*), were not especially effective. Freshly caught, rather than frozen charr, also appeared to be a better bait. Night, or more particularly just before and after dawn, proved the most successful time. The best catch on a single outing was nine Ferox in a night up to 7¾lb in weight. The technique also proved successful at other venues, especially in hydro-electric reservoirs which had no pike population.

We tried several terminal tackle rigs, and as is turning out to be normal in Ferox fishing, the simplest was the best. A free-lined ledger was the least complicated to operate. A freshly caught charr was killed, its swim bladder punctured and a simple hook trace, normally employed in pike dead bait fishing, mounted. We tended to use a six- to eight-inch charr armed with a size six or eight treble hook on the head and middle, finished with a large single hook through the tail wrist. The hooks were pointed to the tail of the fish, the opposite of the position when trolling. This was a lesson learned from pike fishing experience and also from the observation of fish remains in Ferox stomachs. The Ferox, like the pike, tend to swallow their prey head first.

The pick-up of the bait by Ferox was different from my experience of pike. There seems to be a 'swoop and gobble' rather than a mad dash that will drag a rod into the water. The run is very strong and a quick powerful strike against it normally secured the fish. A delayed strike often resulted in a deeply hooked fish that met an obligatory death rather than the option for release. Although a wire trace tackle was used for this type of fishing it was purely a matter of convenience, rather than of necessity. Static dead bait fishing for Ferox would be my primary choice if confined to bank fishing and, after trolling from a boat, is my favourite method of attack. You may even catch the pike of your dreams in addition.

So far I have said comparatively little about flyfishing for Ferox. This is because it is not the premier mode of approach for a fish which is primarily piscivorous. This does not mean to say it can never be effective. Trolled tube flies and tandem lures have been traditionally trolled for Ferox and there

Mr Nicol McIntyre (*left*) ghillie to Mr W. C. Muir in 1866 on the occasion of the capture of the world record (39½lb) trout from Loch Awe. To the right is Mr D. C. Muir, descendant of the captor. Photograph was taken after a day's pike fishing in 1900. (*Lt Col Peyman*)

are several accounts of huge Ferox being taken by this method. Nicol McIntyre, the ghillie who landed the erstwhile rod-caught world record trout of 39½lb from Loch Awe, employed this method to good effect. He did this not only as a young man in 1866 with W.C. Muir, but also some thirty-five years later as an old man ghillie-ing for R.MacDonald Robertson who recorded a tussle with a fly-caught Ferox in the Pass of Brander. He also records in a footnote to his article: 'The largest Ferox known to have been taken in Loch Awe was caught by the late Mr Muir of Inistrynich on a medium-sized salmon fly, the weight being 39½lb. Nicol McIntyre had over forty years of experience on Loch Awe, and presumably his choice of using flies for Ferox was an advised one. Flyfishing purists perhaps would scoff at trolling in this way, but the final fight from a Ferox is not lost by fishing this way. Today's lighter materials and wider range of lures make it an even better prospect than in the past. This is something I am pursuing myself with a range of flies tied, to represent charr fry, by fellow Ferox fanatic Stevie Balmer of Blair Atholl.

Traditional loch-style flyfishing does occasionally produce a surprise Ferox, though it is hardly a standard method of approach. The largest Ferox known by me to be taken in this way was an 11lb fish from Loch Arkaig. The best time for using flies for Ferox seems to be the autumn, when they can also be caught in their spawning rivers. The danger in flyfishing for Ferox is that it can be the slippery slope to an abandonment of that key element, relentlessness. Be warned. I occasionally castigate the bigotry of fly fishermen, but this is a mistake as they are such a useful source of bait!

The 'hows' and the 'whys' of Ferox fishing having been covered, this still leaves the question of where. As someone who lives permanently in the Scottish Highlands I know I am a lucky man. Within a two-hour drive of my home lie some of the best Ferox waters in Europe, if not the world. If you live in Ireland or Cumbria you are also greatly blessed. If you are one of the poor souls who live in the crowded south-east then Ferox fishing is more difficult, short of holiday visits or planned campaigns. One of my friends in the Ferox-85 Group went to the length of buying a timeshare at Loch Rannoch. Now this is what relentlessness really means! However, most of us cannot afford this kind of fanaticism.

The Cumbrian lakes, especially Windermere of course, are perhaps your nearest recourse, or Lake Bala in Wales. Loch Doon in Galloway is also within striking distance if you have come as far as Cumbria. However, it is in the Scottish Highlands and the loughs of Ireland that the dedicated Ferox fisher should set his sights. Here are the great open spaces of lightly fished waters long removed from the lakes of the overcrowded Cumbrian fells. For those wishing to 'cast a longer line' then the Scandinavian lakes and Iceland are a Ferox paradise.

There are too many venues to mention them all individually. In the pantheon of Highland Ferox waters, Quoich, Awe, Arkaig, Assynt, Rannoch, Veyatie and Sionascaig rate highly. These offer the visitor good accommodation as well as good fishing. A plethora of hotels and B&B venues exist if you decide to combine your fishing trip with a family holiday. Rannoch and Awe are especially well-endowed in this way. The Forestry Commission Cabins at Dalavich on Loch Awe offer the best value for money in Ferox-hunter accommodation that I've experienced. Another venue is Loch Quoich which has an excellent hotel nearby, though I cannot recommend the bothies at this place as an exercise in decadence. These three lochs are the most likely lochs I know of to produce a 20lb-plus Ferox.

Of the Scandinavian lakes I am familiar with, Mjøsa and Vattern are the ones with the monster pedigree. A 6lb wild trout in Mjøsa is an average occurrence. These Scandinavian lakes dwarf British waters and are almost inland freshwater seas. Don't be put off – the Ferox are there. One of the main reasons I learned to speak Norwegian was so that I could glean the local knowledge required. Scandinavia is expensive for we 'third world status' Brits, so don't forget the cheaper and shorter journey to Ireland. I have no direct experience of Irish loughs, but the 'Ferox Mafia' inform me that great days may still be had even though the halcyon days of Mask and Corib may be in the past. Lough Erne and Lough Melvin also have great track records for producing huge trout. I look forward to exploring this option myself. Perhaps we might meet. I am the guy with a Scottish accent, a musk ox-fibre balaclava and a bottle of Ferox-85 Group own blend whisky. We can drink a toast to our finny friends the Ferox, and be sure in the knowledge that whether we choose Norway, Ireland, Scotland or Cumbria we will be enjoying one of the finest 'fruits' of the sub-Arctic.

In conclusion we must go back to the basic question of why we go Ferox fishing. I do it because there are no mammoths left. Let's hope the Ferox fare better than their fellows of the frozen past. The future for Ferox is fundamental to us, and how we can help guarantee it now warrants some discussion.

5

Conservation and Management (Ferox forever!)

The purpose of this chapter is to consider the future for Ferox. In the past, Ferox in Britain have survived the vicissitudes of man and nature for at least 12,000 years. They have thus certainly proved their durability by surviving climatic extremes which have seen much colder and much warmer conditions than we have today. They have also survived a long period of exploitation by man, though this has not been on the scale of the salmon and sea-trout fisheries of coastal and inland waters; compared to the halcyon days of Ferox fishing in the last century, they are only lightly exploited at present. Gone are the spear fishing nights on the spawning grounds mentioned by Osgood Mackenzie in his classic book on Highland living. In these days of gloom, doom and despondency on environmental issues, I proffer my neck by saying that in my opinion Ferox have not had it so good for a long time. Right now, in terms of direct pressure, there is no great cause for concern, and we are probably dealing with a largely untapped resource of immense cultural and sporting value. Let us bear in mind though the past follies and abuses that robbed the north and west of the British Isles of much of the rest of their special boreal fauna and make sure that the relatively happy situation that exists today remains so. Problems are better prevented than cured. Complacency is very dangerous and we must never take our Ferox and charr populations for granted. We have already made some mistakes in the past that may have had negative effects on Ferox populations then and now. Removal of the original, largely deciduous native forest, afforestation with exotic conifers and conversion of natural lakes to hydro-electric reservoirs are cases in point.

Mentioning these above points raises the main issue concerning the future for Ferox – that of maintaining the integrity of the environment that produces them. Dr Niall Campbell pointed out that Ferox were associated with a special set of environmental conditions, the main features of which were the occurrence of relatively unproductive lakes of glacial origin which were over 100 hectares in size and also contained Arctic charr. Whatever the latent genetic potential of Ferox is, it can only be expressed in conditions such as these. As long as this type of habitat exists then we have a fair chance of fishing for Ferox 'for ever'. Maintenance of environmental integrity is of the highest priority and takes precedence over any consideration of angling techniques, catch and release arguments or bag limits.

Threats to the integrity of the Ferox and charr environment are regrettably not hard to find. Both these fish are a sub-set of the Arctic-Alpine fauna of northern Europe. As long as the basic bioclimatic profile of the British Isles retains sub-Arctic and boreal features then grounds for optimism on their future exist. Even the warmer conditions of the climatic optimum of 5,000 years ago did not remove them from our faunal list, but we are now faced with the threat of much warmer conditions from the infamous 'Greenhouse effect' of our own making.

The Greenhouse Effect, or rather the postulated outcome of it, is to my mind greatly exaggerated by those engaged in the politics of the latest eco-panic. I am also suspicious of some scientists, who may, in a period of pecuniary stringency, be seeking to secure research funds from the Government by stimulating public concern. The truth remains that due to our modern industrial production systems, successes in meeting the demands of our 'cast-off' consumer society and our indulgent capacity for reproduction, we threaten the basic climate of the globe. Even if we were all able and willing to put up with a lower material standard of living and redressed the most glaring examples of gross pollution of the environment, we are still left with a serious population problem. This is the root cause not only of the Greenhouse Effect, but of other direct and indirect pollution of not only our own environment, but also that of the fish we seek. The most glaring example is of course the disastrous effects of 'acid rain'. If the climate changes in the way the worst Greenhouse Effect predictions suggest, then we can forget about Ferox for a start. Many of us will be too busy with the funeral arrangements in any case. This might improve the population pressure in the long term, but the best option for preventing any further global damage is for more responsibility in family planning. Bearing in mind the amount and type of protective clothing for Ferox fishing I recommended in an earlier chapter then the reader will probably find curbing romantic inclinations easier than the average non-angler.

Acid rain is not a recent problem. There is some evidence to suggest that the problem arose during the great industrial expansion of the eighteenth and especially the nineteenth centuries. At first, during the nineteenth and early twentieth centuries effects were relatively local, probably impacting on upland areas near the industrial centres. The Trossachs, the Pennines, the Lake District and Galloway were probably receiving acidified precipitation last century from the factories of the English Midlands and the central belt of Scotland. After the clean air legislation of the middle of this century we exported our filthy air to other countries, especially Norway. The heightened chimney stacks which followed the change in the law may have prevented the killer smogs of British cities, but they also meant the death sentence for thousands of charr and trout populations in southern Scandinavia. All the more shameful because the Scandinavians had such a relatively clean and unspoiled environment, with little pollution from their own internal sources. Charr are very sensitive to variations in the pH levels of the waters they live in. They are now threatened in Loch Doon because of acid rain, and almost certainly the demise of the Loch Grannoch charr was due to such pollution. Trout populations in other Galloway hill lochs are now under threat. If the charr of Loch Doon disappear then we can say goodbye to the Ferox there, known to reach up to 17lb. This is the last surviving charr population in the southern uplands of Scotland and it supports the only known Ferox population there. My colleague Dr Peter Maitland is now engaged in a major conservation project to save these charr and has introduced them to the Meggat and Talla reservoirs. This seems to have been successful, but such last minute rescue jobs should not be necessary in the first place.

Happily for the Highlands the main area affected by acid precipitation lies to the south and east. Though much wetter than these areas, most of the rainfall in the Highlands is brought in from the Atlantic and avoids passing over the polluted industrial heartlands of Britain and Europe. This is very fortunate indeed considering that the Highlands are the last great refuge for Ferox and charr in mainland Britain. If it were not for this fortunate climatic circumstance then we might have lost large numbers of fish populations in the way that the Scandinavian countries have. The rocks and therefore the lakes and lochs occurring on the bedrock of Scandinavian and British mountains are relatively poor in calcium and have little capacity to neutralise acid rain and snow. This is especially true in spate or spring melt conditions. Fish eggs and emergent fry are very vulnerable to rapid episodic decreases in pH levels, common at such times, and may die. Lakes rich in calcium, lying on lime-rich sedimentary rocks or fertile agricultural areas, buffer fish from the effects of acid rain. It is a matter of luck rather than good judgement that the Highlands and their Ferox populations have largely escaped so far. The effects of acid rain are not always immediate. It may take years before the negative effects manifest themselves, and all too sadly it is often too late for action when they do.

Arguments over acid rain are often linked directly to the debate on the large scale coniferous forests established in the British uplands since World War Two. Conifers in themselves do not cause acid rain, nor in their natural ecosystems do they prevent the development of excellent habitat for salmonid fish. The problem is caused by the way the forests have been planned and managed to meet a small range of strategic aims. Huge areas of densely planted even-aged evergreens act as a very efficient air filter which collects the deposition products of acid rain and concentrates rather than causes the problem. If the acid rain did not exist in the first place then this would not happen to the same degree. This of course does not excuse forestry practice from causing other problems affecting fish populations. This will be commented on later in the chapter.

The problems associated with the Greenhouse Effect and acid rain are derived from pollution from our industrial society, and though the public are aware of them, they do not have the immediate impact of more direct manifestations of pollution, such as smog and the loss of salmon or other fisheries in rivers like the Clyde or Thames. As anglers it is up to us to increase the general awareness of others, because in the end our sport is dependant on a clean environment. That clean environment is also the basis of other people's economic viability, so we have common ground with people who may at times seem to be our enemies.

For centuries the Clyde and Thames supported important fisheries for salmon and sea trout. The salmon had been there for several thousand years and would probably have remained for several thousand more. There was therefore the possibility of millennia of sporting and commercial fishing to support human economies. All this was thrown away to 'make a quick buck' in the Industrial Revolution. However great the short-term wealth created at the time, how can we possibly measure this against the price of the lost fisheries and the lost health of generations of human beings? It does however point out an important lesson that can be applied in other environments. The salmon of the Clyde and Thames were not wiped out by saw-billed ducks, otters, ospreys or seals; nor were they wiped out by netsmen, anglers or fish traps. They were wiped out by the short-sighted greed, ignorance and arrogance of 'industrial man'. When I hear and read the squabbles in the media over seal numbers, the reintroduction of sea eagles and of the relative merits or demerits of catch-and-release angling I am always reminded of an episode in the TV series *Star Trek* where a Klingon warrior reminds Captain Kirk that only fools fight in a burning house. How apt for our present situation.

So far the Ferox and charr waters of the Highlands, Cumbria and much of Ireland have escaped the fate that befell their relatives in southern Britain. Comparatively little of the gross pollution that we associate with lowland waters exists here. This does not mean to say that no problems exist. Windermere has been negatively affected by nutrient enrichment from surrounding urban development. This has been sufficient to change the balance of the fish species. Fertiliser run-off from agricultural holdings has affected Irish waters including the massive Lough Neagh with its special population of pollan and the special race of trout, called dollaghan, which may feed on them. We must also never forget the loss of the Loch Leven charr through manipulation of the water level and industrial development.

Agricultural enrichment has also threatened the viability of the remaining brown trout here. Once again we have to look at this agricultural pollution as a feature of our industrial society; the problem arises from the scale of production and inputs necessary to maintain outputs to large urban markets. However scandalous the damage done in British waters, the pernicious impact of this large-scale pollution is best highlighted and judged by the effects on the Great Lakes of North America. Here whole ecosystems have been wiped out, fish communities devastated and human health and economic systems threatened; yet at one time these waters were vast inland freshwater seas whose bounty, it seemed, would be there for ever. Palpably this was not the case, so what chance for the mere 'puddles' and 'trickles' of the British Isles?

The loss of fisheries brought about by industrial pollution and agricultural enrichment is not just one of commercial or sporting loss, it is also a cultural one. In my childhood and youth the same books which stimulated my interest in Ferox also regaled me with stories of wild and managed brown trout fisheries in England and Wales. There was almost a 'Miss Marple' or 'Sherlock Holmes' English cultural feel about these stories. Although, as a Scotsman, they were not set in an environment which I had direct experience of, they imbued me with a respect and admiration for the appreciation of the wild trout fisheries of my southern cousins. Today I am horrified by the way this lovely tradition has been betrayed and replaced by the commercial development of put-and-take fisheries for reared rainbow trout and stocked brown trout. This instant fishing is to my mind a sheer and utter disgrace to angling in general and the sporting traditions of England in particular. How dare the exponents of this fishing compare the type of so-called flyfishing they do with the traditions of dry and wet flyfishing of the Test and Itchen. As someone who bases the pursuit of his quarry on trolling techniques I cannot claim the way I fish has the subtleties of presenting a dry fly to a rising trout thirty yards away. It may be appropriate for the quarry I seek and it requires its own type of skills and know-how, but there is no way I could support the use of the same language in describing the two approaches. Yet I read, in the southern-based and southern-biased angling press, of people who have caught a tame specimen fish, perhaps only a week out of the stew pond, and described its capture on a 'dead parrot' lashed to a 'billhook' in the same glowing terms as if it were a wild trout caught in the mayfly season on a chalk stream. If the fish concerned had fully developed fins and some skin on its nose it might just be believable, but to my mind still not acceptable. A whole generation has grown up with this sub-culture of angling and has known nothing better. Yet the potential of the English environment for producing good wild trout fisheries is still there. Only abuse, neglect and this kind of piscatorial prostitution stands in the way. The wild trout environment of England has in many places been polluted and urbanised to a point of marginality. It deserves better than the deal it is getting at the moment, and so does the English trout angler.

Regrettably, although the physical pollution is not so widespread, the cultural pollution has also reared its ugly head in Scotland. The situation is morally worse here because it is less excusable. We actually have the situation where anglers from the central belt are travelling to England to fish for stocked rainbows, in what amounts to giant concrete aquariums. Right next door of course, in the Highlands, is some of the best wild brown trout fishing in Europe and some of the most stunning scenery in the world. The lure of the laid-on lunker tempts even in an angling 'Garden of Eden'. Whatever happened to the pursuit of wild burn trout in the hills of home as an induction to angling? It saddens me to think that so many youngsters are missing out on this experience, believing that fish without fins are normal!

Unless there is a full appreciation of the value of our wild fish stocks then we will lose the battle to maintain them. As long as the 'cop out' exists of believing that hand-reared fish in man-made environments will make up for the loss of wild waters, then the threats posed by industrial society remain. This is even true in the fastnesses of the Highlands. The problem here does not arise from put-and-take fisheries *per se*, although these do exist; the danger comes from the industrialisation of fish rearing in the form

Fish rearing units in lochs and sea can cause serious ecological and genetic damage to natural waters. At the industrial scale they are a major hazard in some areas. (*A. F. Walker*)

of the modern aquaculture industry. It is not politically correct these days to criticise this industry, because on the face of it it is good for jobs for the Highlands. However, its present operation, in my opinion, is one of the most potent threats to the ecology and sporting nature of Highland lochs. As a freshwater biologist I have severe doubts over its biological sustainability and it appears to be so inept in its approach to supply and demand market economics that its financial success is also seriously in question also.

Several problems arise from the cage-rearing facilities now present in many Highland lochs. Local pollution from waste food and faecal matter is of course something which comes to mind easily, as does loss of visual amenity. However it is the unseen threats of disease and genetic pollution that are among the most serious threats to wild fish. This has now been worsened by the recent upsurge in interest in rearing charr as an alternative to salmon and rainbow trout. In the harsh conditions of Highland lochs it is not a matter of if, it is a matter of when these fish will escape, by the agency of storm, vandalism or incompetence. Already some fish farmers have shown lack of foresight by importing charr of foreign origins to Scottish lochs. Should these fish then breed with local stock, then a unique genetic inheritance tens of thousands of years in the making will be lost for ever. To whose benefit? Certainly not the charr, Ferox or the anglers who pursue them. Tragically some anglers seem nearly as short-sighted as the fish farmers and take pleasure in capturing huge charr that have grown more rapidly than their ancestors, purely by virtue of living under the cages, feeding on pellets or escaped fry. Technically these are still wild fish, so the criticism levelled at the rainbow 'bashers' does not apply here. How many, though, of the anglers who catch these whopper charr pause after their first flush of success to ponder the long-term impact of what has just happened to them.

A rather sad feature in Highland lochs in recent years has been the development of a sub-culture of fishing for rainbows which have escaped from the 'internment camps' of the aquaculture industry. There is a thriving grape-vine and even occasional press statements indicating the latest piece of bad luck, bad management or vandalism which has released umpteen thousand 'internees' into the real world of multiple dropper set lines, bubble float and maggots and bags of fish pellets to stimulate a 'rise'. I believe there are even 'fly' patterns tied to resemble fish pellets. Well, everyone to their own pleasures I suppose, but what is worrying to me is that these standards come to be applied to wild trout fisheries. For example at Loch Garry, in Highland Perthshire, where a charitable conservation group I am involved with runs the fishery, frequent four-letter-word complaints arise from visiting anglers whose norms are those of proponents of the art of escapee bashing. After catching several dozen rainbow trout at Loch Awe or Loch Tay in a few hours, they believe our loch is fishless if wild trout do not surrender at the first sight of a bunch of worms. It is all very sad really, especially as these poor rainbows are so despicably ugly that among the Ferox-85 Group they are known by the pejorative term 'schumbow'. I believe that there is no long-term future for the fish farming industry as it stands at present. Hopefully it will meet its demise before the long-term future of Ferox, charr and Highland sporting traditions is compromised. I think it is high time for its senior managers and the politicians who back them to sit down and think about the situation. What happened in this Highland industry is part of a sadly repeating pattern of boom-and-bust ventures based on monoculture and run for the benefit of investors in external industrial economies. Forestry, sheep farming and even to some extent sporting estates fall into this category too. All in some way are inimical to the long-term well-being of the Highlands, living as they do off the depleted biological capital of a region rather than its biological interest.

Twenty years ago I began my first study of Arctic charr in the Highlands, at Loch Garry in Perthshire. The loch, now a hydro-electric reservoir, typifies the habitat of Arctic charr in this area of the Grampians. Surrounded by the classic heather moors of popular conception – or perhaps misconception – it enjoys or rather endures an annual temperature regime not markedly unlike Reykjavik in Iceland. Today the habitat is largely treeless, and many people regard this as natural and part of the normality of the Highlands. I believed it then too, but two decades of involvement in conservation issues in the Highlands has long convinced me that this is a long way indeed from the true biological potential of the area. I owe this conversion to the research on the charr population of the loch. As my studies progressed I became more and more aware of the processes that generate the production of the fish population. One of these is the food production cycle sustaining the charr and their main predator, the Ferox; just as on land, all the higher animal production is based directly and indirectly on plant production, itself the link to the energy supply from the sun. In hydro-electric reservoirs this pathway is severely disrupted by water level fluctuations destroying plant life in the littoral zone, the most productive part of such lochs. Swedish research indicates that in such situations up to seventy per cent of the production of invertebrate animals, the main food of trout and charr, can be lost. Needless to say, this is not good news for anglers let alone the fish.

Through other work, by my then colleagues at the Freshwater Fisheries Laboratory at Pitlochry, I became aware of the fact that in upland stream and lake ecosystems most of the plant material which supports the food organisms of fish such as trout, juvenile salmon and charr is not derived from the internal resources of the water. The main source of plant material enters from the surrounding landscape, most obviously in the form of autumn-shed leaves. In waters of low natural productivity up to ninety per cent of the plant material may come from this source, and even in productive waters sometimes as much as two thirds. In total terms we are talking several tons of leaf litter per hectare being added each year. The processing of this leaf litter in the aquatic ecosystem has, in some ways, more in common with the compost heap than with another analogy of caterpillars eating leaves and forming the food of birds. In the stream or lake the processing is carried out by plant scavengers, or detritivores to give them their technical term. Juvenile Ferox depend heavily on these consumers of dead plants for their own food and any depression of production of this food source should be viewed with concern by those who seek the fish. This is exactly what has happened in hydro-electric reservoirs, and while these types of waters remain excellent charr habitat containing a rich food source for those Ferox who make the grade, there is a more difficult early period with reduced production of trout in general. This would probably be much less of a problem if there was an alternative source of plant material to the aquatic plants, destroyed by water level changes. In natural circumstances there would of course be a forest to do exactly that. The British uplands have, of course, not been natural for thousands of years. They are in fact a cultural landscape created by our own agrarian and pastoral land use practices. The single largest impact in the creation of this cultural landscape has been the removal of the original native forest, which was largely deciduous in nature. The British Isles are among the least forested areas of Europe. In Scotland we are now down to the last one per cent of the original forested land. England, Wales and Ireland are little different. Even Iceland has a greater area of native forest than Scotland. There are many downsides to this forest removal, but one which as anglers we should be acutely aware of is the loss of productivity of fishing waters. One of the biggest fisheries management problems we face in managing Ferox and charr waters is current land use. Thankfully this too is gaining recognition and riparian owners are beginning to reappraise the potential benefits of sound woodland management in their catchment areas. Recent developments in the River Findhorn and River Dee watersheds are an encouraging example.

Subsistence peasant agrarian/pastoral production systems pose little threat in this sense and the fact that as far is as known no Ferox or charr populations were ever lost because of the land use practices or harvesting techniques of native local people is an indication of this. One possible exception is the charr of St Mary's Loch in Selkirkshire, which may have been over-harvested. However, it is not this form of agriculture that caused the problem. The present upland sheep farming system which many people consider traditional is nothing of the kind and is scarcely a few centuries old. It was instituted to supply a product to the industrial south. Now heavily subsidised, it would not be capable of standing on its own merits in today's market economy. The price we are paying for this stupidity is more than just a financial one. It is an upland environment shorn of its true biological, and therefore its true economic potential.

Yet the sheep are not alone to blame for the loss of this potential. The total package of grouse moor and deer 'forest' management adds salt to the wound. The whole quasi-feudal Victorian anachronism may help sell a mass of shortbread tins, but it is selling the Highlands short including their wonderful salmonid fisheries. One wonders just how many millions of salmon smolts over the centuries have been lost to reduced productivity, not to mention charr and Ferox production losses. It's all part of the unseen price we pay for what the famous ecologist Sir Frank Fraser Darling once described as a 'wet desert'. This 'unspoiled' rugged grandeur we are selling to tourists is to my mind nothing of the kind. It is little more than an ecological slum, beautiful in spite of what has been done to it more than because of it. Erosion scars are dramatic to look at, but sad if you are aware that the silt washed out from them ends up in a spawning stream for Ferox or salmon. All these things have happened because a basic biological truth has been ignored. The one and only true resource from which all our activities are based, including fishing for Ferox, is the soil and vegetation complex that accesses for higher organisms the sunlight energy which drives the whole system. The sheep, the grouse and the deer are not the

Re-establishment of deciduous woodland in the riparian area of upland waters could be of major benefit in the British Isles. (*Loch Garry Tree Group*)

Members of the Loch Garry Tree Group gather for a tree planting outing in typically sub-arctic weather. Changing a landscape to help ferox and charr can be a chilly business! (*Lee Stradmeyer*)

resource; they are only mechanisms we employ to render the resource available for our man-made cash economy. We have failed so far to meet the challenge of managing that true resource. Eventually we will cause the system to collapse unless we change our ways, and we will lose more than just the fishing. The time is right for restoring the main component of the soil-vegetation complex, the forest. For me this is no esoteric, ethereal or abstract concept. At Loch Garry a process of re-establishment of deciduous woodland has been in force for twenty years, and all because I wanted more fish! In addition work on the establishment of perennial plants, tolerant of periodic inundation, in the draw-down zone of the loch is being carried out to assist the accruing benefits offered by tree leaf-litter. If you feel the same way, get out there and plant some deciduous trees.

Talking about reforestation in the uplands of the British Isles usually conjures up nightmares of serried ranks of monocultural madness, a 'disease' for which I have coined the expression 'Sitkaphrenia' to cover the cellulose factory approach of post-war British forestry. Whatever else these huge areas of Sitka spruce and Lodgepole pine purport to be, they are definitely not true forests. True boreal forest provides a good habitat for fish in the water systems surrounded by it: it helps stabilise water flows and run-offs; it traps sunlight energy and transfers it to aquatic ecosystems via its deciduous species; it can modify water temperatures during climatic extremes and provide cover and protection for fish in streams.

What has been created in the British uplands is a few components of the boreal forest without the diversity of either species or structure of the original and the benefits it offered to aquatic habitat. The establishment and harvesting techniques so frequently used to date, far from rendering a fish-friendly forest to us are actually inimical to the well-being fish stocks in several important ways. I say 'to date' advisedly because there are positive signs that the Forestry Authority is moving to a higher degree of environmental responsibility, and the days when 'unreconstructed' foresters roamed the earth seems to be coming to an end. The same cannot always be said for the private sector and sub-contractors hired to carry out specific operations. Forestry being what it is, even at its best it is a long-term activity. We are still living with the mistakes of forty years ago and fish populations have been and still are negatively affected. From planting to harvest, disruption of fish habitat occurs when the forest is managed in the cellulose factory manner. Prior to planting, one of the most common preparations has been the ploughing of furrows vertically through, rather than along the contours of hills. Frequently in the past these furrows connected or came very close to streams and rivers. The result was an increased run-off of silt, during spates, in river systems, silt which could suffocate the spawning redds of salmon and trout. Some of these streams were Ferox spawning sites. Subsequent planting on this ploughed land, frequently in the past, was right up to the stream edges. Later in the forest cycle this caused deep shade which cut out the life-giving light both to the stream itself and the riparian undergrowth which helped stabilise the stream banks. There was also heavy input of conifer needles, which are a very poor source of food material compared to leaves. The result was fish nursery streams stripped of most of their rearing capacity for juvenile fish.

Things are gradually changing for the better and there now exist excellent working guidelines for commercial forestry to avoid these gross errors of the past. These are fine in theory, but they have to be rigorously applied and I am aware of sad incidents where they have been ignored. In the long term there are still the problems of strategic water balance changes and extraction procedures as the forests established decades ago come into their main production cycles. There is a mass of North American and European literature pointing out the guidelines for timber extraction that does not destroy riparian habitat. The main requirement is for a buffer region where riparian trees remain in perpetuity felled on a selection rather than clear-fell basis. The wrong type of timber harvesting can ruin stream habitat for spawning fish. We must be careful in the future and not be lulled into the complacency of thinking that just because we have identified the risk we have obviated the problem. Nationally we are now into low double percentage figures of land covered in these 'new forests'. Regionally, such as in places like Argyll and Galloway, about half the area is forest. By simple deduction this means that many miles of possible trout and salmon nursery streams are in catchment areas dominated by conifer forest. We have much to lose if the forest management is not harmonious with the habitat requirements of fish. In the long term we have to ask ourselves what kind of national forest we need and what we expect from it. As a trout angler I expect prime riparian habitat of a mixed open forest, mainly of light shade-casting trees, and shrubs. Dominated by native deciduous trees it would alternate with small open glades with diverse wetland, grassland and herb communities; in some ways very like the habitat created by beavers in the past. In fact, why not let beavers do the job for us? Beavers bring their own management responsibilities of course, but they are a keystone species in aquatic environments. Despite occasional access problems they are an aquatic asset. Beavers or not, the national forest estate is not one with which at present we as anglers can feel at ease. Its strategic management is of primary importance in maintaining wild game fish stocks. Falling leaves are future Ferox.

I hope by this stage in the book you have realised that fish do not live in a vacuum. They of course live in an environment, as you do. I am always amazed by the way some anglers divorce themselves from this reality and immerse themselves so strongly in their chosen pursuit that they forget the fact that it is no use trying to argue over the niceties of catching fish by this or that method if the habitat which produces the fish is rendered unsuitable. Do not feel too badly about this if you are such an angler. I have met quite a few fish biologists, especially in senior management, who to me seemed to think that fish were the only animals which did not live in an environment. Acid rain and Chernobyl to some extent were a blessing in disguise. Prior to this, tagging and scale reading seemed to be the be all and end all of fisheries research, especially if salmon were the subject matter. People like me who were Ferox freaks, environmental enthusiasts and charr fanatics were regarded as dangerous dissidents. The sacrifice of my career was made worthwhile when I found out that a certain ex-boss of mine is now spouting my advice and breaking sweat planting trees in his new life as a consultant. We even share a detestation of hill sheep farming.

Several times I have made passing reference to the development of natural lochs into hydro-electric reservoirs. This environmental change, though less important than the macro-environmental scale of the above considerations of atmospheric pollution on the industrial scale, is of much more immediate direct effect on charr and Ferox populations. The conversion of a natural lake to a hydro-electric reservoir marks the biggest physical change in the lake environment since the end of the Ice Age. The biological effects are profound, frequently negative and mostly irreversible. This does

The establishment of vegetation in the draw-down zone of hydro-electric reservoirs is very challening but could offer major benefits to fish populations. (*Dr C. D. Strange*

not mean *per se* that such usage is a totally bad thing. The production of energy to meet the needs of our industrial society involves some kind of environmental cost. That cost may be acid rain from the burning of fossil fuels, leukaemia and other cancers from nuclear sources or the loss of biological productivity in lakes. Each production method costs human lives in accidents and of course takes substantial cash inputs to maintain. Hydro-electric power production has few of the health and pollution problems associated with other methods. Probably only solar and wind energy is cleaner in this respect. If you do not like any of them then remember you are part of the problem. Your energy demands are creating the need for power production. I am guilty too of course, and the word processor I typed this book on is plugged into the national grid. I daresay my power demands have done more damage to trout and charr populations than my netting or angling activities. I wonder how many words it takes to kill a fish?

The price fish pay for living in one of our reservoirs is a high one, but there are also new opportunities and stimuli to research. Without the challenge of hydro-electric development the corpus of scientific knowledge on charr and Ferox, especially in Scandinavia, would be much smaller.

When the prospect of the dried-up river bed of the Perthshire Garry greets you from the A9 on the way north to Inverness, it is not difficult to imagine the profound effects this may have had on the spawning areas for salmon. Reduced access to migratory fish has been one of the main criticisms levelled at hydro-electric development in Britain. Whatever the scale of the problem in this country, it pales to insignificance in comparison with what has happened in Fennoscandia. Hardly any major river systems in Norway and Sweden remain unaffected by hydro-electric regulation. Almost all the natural salmon smolt production of Sweden has been detrimentally affected and hatchery production of smolts is on a colossal scale. Though most of the political concern has been with regard to the negative effects on salmon runs there is also growing concern about the effects on the large fish-eating trout of the great Scandinavian lakes whose spawning areas have also been lost. This spawning ground loss and the inimical changes in the productivity of the littoral nursery areas for young Ferox in the lakes concerned means that the Ferox-producing potential has been greatly reduced. There are now major Ferox rehabilitation schemes in progress involving a wide range of sporting, social and conservation organisations in a combined attack on the problem. These schemes are exemplified by specific management projects in the lakes Tyrifjord and Mjøsa in Norway and Vänern in Sweden. The waters concerned are among the most famous Ferox lakes in Scandinavia, which sadly were threatened from a number of directions. The main threats were to the spawning and nursery areas.

Lake Vänern in Sweden, with a surface area in excess of 5,500 square kilometres, is so large compared to British still-waters that it is almost best considered as an inland freshwater sea. Among a great many other biological points of interest it contains a population of landlocked salmon which feed on the whitefish populations, (powan, smelt etc.), and a race of Ferox which behave like landlocked sea trout and which are likewise piscivorous. Both the salmon and the trout have been recorded as reaching weights of twenty kilograms and there are unconfirmed reports of Ferox in excess of twenty-seven kilograms (almost 60lb); the average size of the spawning adults is seven to eight kilograms. Fish of this quality are obviously an important fisheries resource, but unfortunately they have been adversely affected by the hydro-electric impoundment of the spawning river, the Gullspång. So closely are these fish associated with this river that they are called colloquially the Gullspång salmon and the Gullspång trout. They are important commercial and sporting resources of great value to the local community. Their fast growth and good recapture rate after stocking has also made them of value to other lakes. Damming of the river has altered the flow and substrate character so fundamentally that since the 1960s great concern has been expressed over their long-term well-being, when there appeared to be a substantial reduction in their numbers. The loss of natural spawning grounds initiated a major rehabilitation scheme

involving the Swedish fisheries authorities at Jonkoping and the private
power company Gullspång Kraft AB. This was a massive undertaking
involving thousands of tons of rock and gravel in the construction of new
spawning areas and a scientific study of the after-effects. Dr Arne Johlander
reported positive benefits from this in his paper presented to the Nordic
Seminar on the Management of Races of Large Trout held in Lillehammer in
1991. Encouraging as this may be there still remains the fact that the original
habitat of the trout has been radically altered by industrial development.
The aquatic environment in the original rearing areas has been permanently
altered in a way that now favours predatory fish such as pike and there is
now a predation pressure on the descending trout and salmon smolts that
did not exist before damming.

Similar problems along with the additional ones of pollution and over-
exploitation have also affected the Ferox of the Norwegian lakes Mjøsa and
Tyrifjord. These are respectively the largest (362km) and the fifth largest,
(139km) lakes in Norway and two of the most famous Ferox waters in the
country. Mjøsa has produced trout over twenty kilograms in weight, and
because of its position in the relatively densely populated south of the
country is an important fishery both commercially and recreationally. This
very location however has been the root cause of a dramatic decline in the
trout stocks. Pollution, water level regulation and canalisation of the main
spawning stream brought about by damming has caused a worrying
decline in the trout population. Central to this decline has been the loss
of spawning streams. Norwegian scientists Morten Kraaboll and Jo Arnek-
leiv reported in the 1991 seminar that half of the original forty spawning
streams had been seriously damaged by the 1970s, though some recent
improvement in the last few years had been noticeable. Most of these
streams had genetically distinct trout populations including the main
Ferox-producing stream, the 197 kilometre-long River Gudbrandalslagen.
Lake Mjøsa itself has been the subject of a series of water level changes by
construction of dams since the late nineteenth century, but the main
problem to the Ferox spawning areas in the Gudbrandalslagen occurred
in 1963 when power development took place at the Hunderfossen and
Ensbyfallene waterfalls. The spawning areas just immediately below and
above the former site have earned the Ferox the title of the Hunder trout.
The site now includes a fish pass and trap which has been very useful in
collecting data on the spawning fish, but which at high water levels does
not attract fish. Nevertheless it has helped create a valuable database of
which fish scientists in this country would be envious.

The decline of the Ferox fishery in Mjøsa became a social and political
issue as much as a biological one. This sparked a major improvement
project termed 'Operation Mjøsa Trout'. The project has a five-year remit to
look at a variety of management protocols and initiatives to ensure the

survival of the Ferox. Central to this has been a collaborative effort of local/ national private and public organisations to secure strategic aims in the long-term management of the Ferox resource and the tactical practicalities in realising this. Key points in this are a major stocking programme of 40,000 2-year-old trout annually, habitat improvement measures and the organisation, regulation and promotion of the fishery on sound biological principles.

A similar project has also been set up on Lake Tyrifjord. This has been brought about by the threat to two separate races of Ferox in the lake. One race of Ferox is an outflow spawner using the River Drammen and the other the main inflowing stream, the River Rand. There are considerable differences in the two forms. The River Rand Ferox reach weights of up to fifteen kilograms (33lb) whilst the River Drammen stock 'only' attain maximum sizes of around six to seven kilograms. Growth increments in the bigger Ferox form can be up to one kilogram per year even in this relatively unproductive water.

The threat here comes from similar environmental degradation as at the other lakes, together with over-harvesting by netting and angling and predation/competition from pike and other coarse fish species. Recruitment of the Ferox has been severely affected and a series of management measures has been promulgated to rectify the situation. Central to this again is the involvement of local communities, private business concerns and public institutions. Hand in hand with the direct protection of the resource is a protocol for allowing the sporting and commercial harvesting of the trout to remain an important local economic base. Tactics again involve a major stocking programme, habitat improvement measures, regulation of fishing methods, (both netting and angling) and a promotion of the intrinsic, social and economic value of the Ferox resource. The stocking programme envisaged will cost more than one million kroner (about £120,000), with the aim of trebling the population of trout to provide an annual catch of between six and nine tonnes.

I can imagine that the stocking programmes mentioned above have struck accord with a good number of readers. In some of your hearts there is probably a feeling of 'never mind all this environmental rubbish, let's get down to the nitty-gritty of putting more fish in the bucket'. I am well acquainted with this attitude and it never ceases to amaze me why so many anglers perceive stocking to be the panacea to end the misery of blank days. Well blank days are a normal feature of Ferox fishing, and even in these Scandinavian paradises anglers can come home with as many Ferox as points scored by some Norwegian entries of the past in the Eurovision song contest. Blank days are bad, but if they are not in your tolerance range, then, as I have already advised, forget about Ferox fishing.

In a sense stocking is a monument to failure. The ideal situation is to have an intact resource with all the main feeding and spawning areas for Ferox capable of sustaining the population at its optimum natural level. The stocking projects outlined above are, if you remember, a response to degraded natural situations and were part of a holistic approach to improving them. A quick-fix fish is not part of the strategy. There is no room for a major stocking programme in a natural lake in prime condition. Just be glad to take the bounty it offers and do not try to excuse any lack of success you may encounter by saying there are too few fish.

However, in lake ecosystems disturbed by our greed and ignorance there may well be a place for stocking in the management strategy. In this we can draw, especially in the hydro-electric reservoirs of the Scottish Highlands, on the experience of our Scandinavian cousins. In such scenarios the loss of spawning, especially in the outflows may have been a serious blow to recruitment of Ferox. We of course do not have the classic before-and-after studies of the Fennoscandian nations on the effects of this, but there is a strong *a priori* case for some concern; Loch Rannoch, Loch Awe possibly, and the Perthshire Loch Garry certainly, being such cases. On top of the loss of spawning, the more difficult conditions presented by the loss of prime feeding habitat for juvenile Ferox in the littoral zone are likely to have negatively affected recruitment to the 'true' Ferox stage. On the other, positive, hand the usual development of a huge population of stunted fodder fish in hydro-modified lakes creates a very useful potential Ferox food source. This is the classic 'double indemnity' that can justify a Ferox stocking project. Reduced recruitment and a food surplus potential were the main biological driving forces behind the Tyrifjord and Mjøsa trout restoration schemes.

There is therefore a reasonable case for considering that stocking of Ferox would be an appropriate management tool in certain situations in British waters, especially in upland hydro-electric reservoirs. Before its use would be justified a more detailed database on the present populations of both Ferox and prey fish would be required. Already however there are some indications that a number of Ferox waters have lost spawning areas and that substantial populations of small-sized charr exist. There appears to be a great deal of similarity in the overall effects of damming on the structure of Ferox and charr populations in Scottish and Scandinavian lake-reservoirs and it is likely that we could draw heavily on the experience and management principles of Nordic research in constructing protocols for our own situations. The kind of stocking envisaged above is in no biological, or indeed moral, way equivalent to the instant whopper approach taken by some English fisheries that I railed against so strongly earlier. What is being contemplated in the approach postulated for lake reservoirs is a replacement for the more difficult 'apprentice' Ferox phase in the littoral or nursery stream prior to the fish-eating journeyman stage. By the actions of changing the lake environment we cause an already difficult situation to become worse and it does not seem unreasonable to do something about it. By rearing local origin wild fish to a size where they would naturally turn to eating fish we are obviating a problem of our own creation. Thereafter the fish lives in a natural way unlike its southern 'equivalent' reared in a pond until a few days before its capture.

Stocking, as I have said earlier, is something of an admission of failure. Usually the basic problem is something that man has done. There are of course many small lochans in the Highlands which have poor natural spawning areas, and without intervention would not provide useful sport. It is even more true that there are huge numbers of places where recruitment levels are very good, even too good from an angling viewpoint, and stocking is not necessary at all.

Unfortunately stocking has become almost an article of faith and somehow or other fishery owners or angling clubs feel that they are letting the side down if there is not a reasonable annual 'dump' of fish to assuage either the concerns or greed of members. This attitude is welcomed by hatchery owners as their business is supplying this need. Stimulating the need is, of course, good for business! If angling clubs can afford it then one of the most frequent management practices seems to be the establishment of a club hatchery. This starts off with a wave of intense enthusiasm followed by a general fall-off of support, leaving a few long-suffering individuals to shoulder the burden. It is difficult in this situation to provide an economically or ecologically sound service to the fishery. Stocking may give a false impression of doing good; it is often useless and sometimes even worse than useless. It is not an option to be entered into lightly. Stock in haste and repent until the next Ice Age might be a useful version of the usual proverb on marriage.

Trout as a species are morphologically, ecologically and genetically diverse. This diversity is an asset not to be dismissed lightly. After all, it is expressed in the existence of our prized Ferox. Ferox from different localities can be very different from one another, and even within the one lake more than one stock may exist. Lake Tyrifjord is a case in point. They also may, of course, be different from the other forms of trout which share their lake. Any stocking programme which does not recognise this is morally bankrupt and should not be entered into. One of the main recommendations of the Nordic seminar describing the Scandinavian stocking trials mentioned above is that it is of prime importance to recognise the separate entity of each of these sub-populations within any lake and not to cross-breed them for release into the home or any other lake. It is also important to recognise that any selection of fish from any individual sub-group of trout for providing hatchery stock may be very narrow, and may not reflect the total genetic diversity of the group.

Constant breeding from a limited number of hatchery-held brood stock is not advisable.

This places logistical constraints on any would-be angling club hatchery manager, and there is a constant temptation to ignore the protocol or buy in domesticated stock; this latter point was earmarked as something to be avoided in the Scandinavian experience, as was the introduction of wild stock from other water systems. The Scandinavians have made mistakes in this respect, so hopefully we can learn from their experience. Sadly I have already seen similar mistakes made here also, and by people who should have known better too (including myself).

If a Ferox enhancement scheme is to be considered after taking into account the above concerns then we can draw yet further on the lessons learned by our Nordic friends. One of the key lessons was that it is useless putting Ferox origin fish into lakes without substantial populations of suitably sized prey fish. In the survey work carried out in the Norwegian lakes Tyrifjord, Randsfjord and Mjøsa, population estimates of potential prey fish up to the size of twenty centimetres were approximately 250, 600, and 750 per hectare, equivalent to between a half a million to one-and-a-half million prey fish in a lake the size of Loch Rannoch. Even this is thought to be an underestimate. Such a plentiful supply of small- to medium-sized prey items is essential for a successful Ferox enhancement stocking scheme.

Perhaps the scientist with most experience with regard to stocking trials with Ferox is my friend, tutor and colleague Dr Per Aass of the Zoological Museum of Oslo. With the benefit of a lifetime's work with various origins of Ferox, especially from Lake Tunhovdfjord and Mjøsa, his experiences in an environment much like the one we might have to manage more wisely, offer much food for thought.

I can still remember the pleasure, astonishment and sheer awe that filled me when I saw my first Ferox in Norway – a 24lb hen fish captured in the spawning river of Tunhovdfjord to provide eggs for the enhancement project and origin trials in Norwegian lakes. I did not need any convincing that this fish was a representative of a very special breed. Tunhovd trout are famous in Norway, largely through the work of Dr Aass. The study of their ecology has been instrumental in providing insights into the Ferox phenomenon and guidelines for their future management.

Much of the work of Dr Aass has centred round the Ferox of Lake Tunhovd and Lake Mjøsa. Tunhovdfjord has a regulation level in excess of sixty feet, and the resulting formation of extensive charr spawning grounds in the barren draw-down zone and the loss of production of aquatic invertebrates has created a large population of stunted charr. Only about one charr in 30,000 attains a length in excess of thirty centimetres. Both the current environmental situation and the presence of charr are the result of human impact. Prior to the end of World War One, Tunhovd was a natural lake about the size of Windermere or Loch Tummel. Impoundment of eighteen metres occurred in 1919/20 increasing the surface area to a size slightly bigger than Loch Rannoch. Originally the lake contained only trout. The average capture size of these was about a pound, with some individuals reaching weights of 4½-6½lb. Scientific studies around this time indicated that fish were not an important feature of their diet. Not long after, regulation charr and minnows entered from other waters in the man-made watershed. The charr entered from the high altitude trout lake, Breivatn, where they had been introduced about a decade previously and had caused a severe reduction in the trout population.

A certain section of the trout of Tunhovd however responded to the changed conditions in an exciting way. Huge trout of up to sixteen kilograms (35lb) first appeared in the late 1930s. Investigation of trout stomachs revealed that nearly all fish over twenty-five centimetres had become almost exclusively piscivorous. It had seemed as if Ferox had appeared from nowhere. Of course they had not, it just meant that there was a latent genetic potential for the trout of Tunhovd to become Ferox if the situation presented itself. In this sense Tunhovd trout do not meet the working Scandinavian definition of Stororret (Great trout), being a piscivorous fish with a running-water juvenile phase followed by an obligatory habitat shift to pelagic predator in adult life. However, they are still a good working definition of the kind of trout that many of us would like to have on the end of our lines! The Tunhovd scenario, natural and man-made, has implications for management of our own Ferox waters and is worth paying attention to.

'Facilitative' Ferox these fish may be, but the genetic component in their make-up was vindicated by later stocking trials which made them one of the most sought after origins in Norway. Natural recruitment of the large trout is very limited and fish are collected each season in the River Numedalslagen for brood stock for the enhancement scheme and stocking trials. In Tunhovd alone over 800,000 fish have been used in the stocking study to date. Recapture rates, depending on the size and age of the stocked fish, have resulted in the proportion of stocked fish in the annual catch being between twenty-three and forty-three per cent. Significantly it has produced a greater proportion of Ferox origin fish in the catch. In terms of the costs involved in the production and release of the young fish the financial return, with regard to the sales value of the fish flesh is minimal. This may be of no significance in Britain compared to a country like Norway where inland fisheries are still an important component of the rural economy. However this does not detract from the scientific value of the experiment nor to the other value concepts surrounding sports fishing. The fact is that the stocking worked very well as a management tool.

In other experiments carried out by Dr Aass, Tunhovd Ferox have also been stocked in a variety of other waters, with varying degrees of success. Not surprisingly, when introduced to waters with large populations of stunted charr they performed very well. A good example of this was in the Silset reservoir on the Molde peninsula. This lake had a population of stunted adult charr weighing around twenty to the kilogram. The local trout were also very small and did not prey extensively on the charr. Tunhovd Ferox were stocked at densities of ten and five fish per hectare using one-summer-old and one-year-old fish respectively. After five to six years the introduced fish comprised more than thirty per cent of the annual catch with the Tunhovd-origin fish, unlike the local trout, preying on the charr and later attaining weights of up to six to seven kilograms.

Even more spectacular success was obtained in the reservoir Lake Rodungen, where the prey fish consisted again of stunted charr and also powan. Natural recruitment of the local trout here is very limited. Tunhovd trout were introduced and quickly turned to charr and then powan for prey. The stocked fish constituted eighty per cent of catch returns and reached weights of between eight and ten kilograms. Encouraging, but much less dramatic results were also obtained in Lake Gopollen. Here the prey fish were minnows and stunted powan. As well as Tunhovd trout, origins from

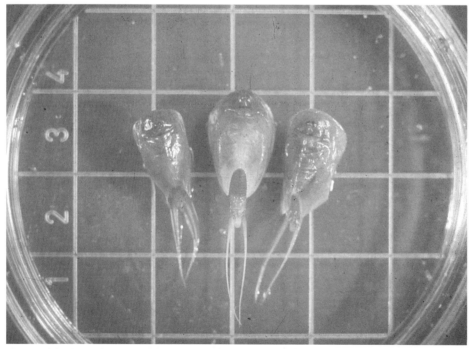

The 'tadpole' shrimp – *Lepidurus Arcticus*. The grid on the dish is one centimetre square. This crustacean is valuable trout and charr food in Arctic and sub-Arctic lakes. No major ecological problems have been associated with its introduction to new waters (*Per Aass*)

Lake Bjornes, and Lake Istern were tried. Tunhovd trout again gave the best returns, though with no especially huge fish being reported. Even in some situations where there were no substantial prey fish populations Tunhovd trout have out-performed local trout. This was the case in Lake Starsjø, where chironomid larvae and the tadpole shrimp, *Lepidurus arcticus*, were the primary prey organisms, and Lake Sonsevatn, where again bottom-living invertebrates were the main food items. In both situations Tunhovd trout grew faster than the local forms as well as being in better condition and having superior flesh quality. They did not however reach the large sizes recorded where they had the possibility of becoming true Ferox. These varying, but mainly very successful, stocking trials all took place in mountain lake-reservoirs situated at altitudes between 300 and 1,400 metres above sea level and with relatively simple fish communities dominated by salmonid species. In more lush locations such as Lake Katnosa, near Oslo, where more complicated fish communities existed, including coarse fish species such as perch, results were not so positive. Seven years after the introduction of Tunhovd trout here the largest fish reported in the official catch returns was scarcely over a pound though one of over two kilograms (4.4lbs) was reported later. Hardly encouraging though, compared to the mountain-lake experiences. The main problem seems to have been caused by negative interaction with the perch.

A further indication of the unsuitability of Tunhovd Ferox for stocking in lowland waters with diverse fish communities came from stocking trials in Lake Mjøsa carried out in conjunction with other stocking trials involving the local Hunder trout. None of the spectacular results with Tunhovd trout in mountain lakes materialised, despite the apparently abundant food supply of suitably sized smelt, *Osmerus eperlanus* (the same species occa-sionally found in British estuarine waters). Recaptures indicated that few Tunhovd fish had managed to access the pelagic zone of the lake, and prey on the smelt there. Dr Aass concluded that the Tunhovd Ferox was behaviourally maladapted for life in places like Mjøsa. Essentially it performed well where the main prey was bottom-living charr, or at least charr with a bottom-living phase in its annual life cycle. Excellent as was its performance in low productivity mountain lakes, its bottom-feeding pre-ferences were not well suited to lakes where the main prey species occupied the open mid-water zone.

Lake Mjøsa Ferox on the other hand showed all the quintessential features of the criteria of being the Scandinavian Great Trout. The Hunder trout stock live as river residents for about four years then migrate as 'smolts' when they reach a length of about twenty-five centimetres (ten inches). They then spend between two and four years as lake resident fish predators before returning as first time spawners. In contrast to the Lake Tunhovd 'facilitative' Ferox they have been specific, well adapted, pelagic

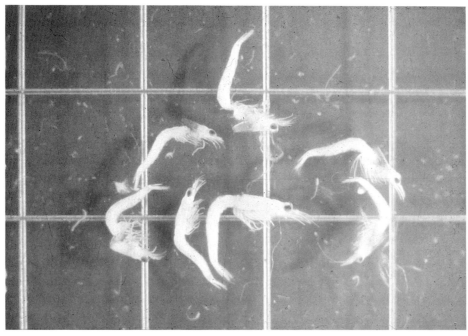

The 'oppossum shrimp' *Mysis Relicta*. An excellent food organism for trout and charr, but introduction to new waters causes major ecological problems. It should *not* be introduced to British lakes. (*Per Aass*)

piscivores for many thousands of years and thus prodigious consumers of the open water smelt. On this rich diet they can, before the onset of sexual maturity, increase in length annually by ten to fifteen centimetres. The loss of such a valuable resource through the effects of damming was considered by the Norwegians to be very serious indeed, hence the major stocking enhancement scheme.

Again, well over 800,000 fish have been used in the stocking programme. In the period 1973–91 alone, between 17,000 and 74,000 River Hunder origin trout were stocked annually to offset the effects of damming. The overall stocking rate has been about one smolt per two hectares, giving a return of 750g per 1,000 stocked. Not immediately a cause for excitement at first glance to an angler, but it now means that over fifty per cent of the trout caught in Mjøsa are derived from the stocking initiative. A remarkable achievement indeed considering that many marked fish are not reported by anglers and that up to ten per cent of the stocked fish have lost their tags. As well as indicating the basic success of the stocking programme, much information on the effects of timing of release, point of release and size at release has come to light. Ideally the stocked fish should be reared to a size where they can immediately access fish as food, rather than going through an invertebrate-eating phase. Funnily enough this is at about twenty-five centimetres, the normal size for a wild smolt. However, production costs being what they are, this is not always easy to achieve.

Wild smolts are the optimum production unit for future Ferox and the stocked fish are a second-best substitute. Though stocked fish grew at the same rate as the wild fish in Mjøsa, the larger size at emigration to the lake of the wild fish conferred a considerable advantage later in life. Of adult fish returning to spawn, only three per cent of hatchery derivation exceeded seven kilograms. This compares with fifteen per cent for the wild origin fish. The growth rate of the smolts when they reach the lake and become active Ferox is prodigious. The three-, four-and five-year-old smolts can reasonably be expected to reach within three years of lake life weights of 2.6, 2.9 and 3.5 kilograms respectively. Mjøsa trout are very well adapted to their own situation or to very similar ones. They do not perform very well in small mountain lakes, and although some individuals have attained large sizes in such situations, no new Ferox population has been established from their introduction.

The biological lessons from the work of Dr Aass and other Scandinavian scientists are of prime importance in reflecting on our own situation. It would be less than wise – bearing in mind the variation found from one Ferox strain to another, both 'inter-lake 'and intra-lake' – to judge all British Ferox by the same yardstick. The Ferox of Lough Neagh would appear to have some general parallels with those of Lake Mjøsa in that they inhabit an extensive water body where the main food item is the pelagic pollan. The comparisons are more complicated in places like Rannoch, where there are both pelagic and benthic charr as potential prey. This begs the question whether or not there may be sub-divisions of the Ferox here as there are in Lake Tyrifjord. Do we have inflow and outflow spawning Ferox with different feeding habits? What is the long-term future for Ferox in Windermere bearing in mind its substantial coarse fish populations? These and many other questions will go unanswered until we take the same interest in our Ferox that our Scandinavian counterparts have, both as scientists and anglers.

Here we are, with one of the least utilised and least studied groups of Ferox populations in Europe. We are richly endowed with them. Any other country in Europe would probably be very proud of them and commit substantial resources to studying and utilising them. What do we do with them? Well we write them off as 'ugly toothy tadpoles' of little or no sporting value, only fit for the despised technique of trolling. Such is the British ignorance of this magnificent fish. This is only a general statement of course and there are those who do know better, but not yet enough.

The Ferox enhancement programmes of Scandinavia are part of a generally better awareness there of environmental issues. In the experiments involved in the trials outlined earlier the social commitment is immense, involving a wide range of community and economic interests. From schools to scientific and business establishments Ferox are part of the local culture. Compared to this scenario we are living in the Dark Ages. It is time that we treated our Ferox populations more seriously and gave them the respect that is long overdue. In Ferox we have a very special resource indeed, and one for a change that is more abundant in the economically more marginal areas of the country. Even with the addition of the Scandinavian nations to the European Union there is no Ferox mountain of over-production. Ferox angling could generate some much needed economic input to the remoter areas of the British Isles, notwithstanding the blandishments of the anti-angling lobby. With free access between the countries in the new Europe this undiscovered 'gold mine' will probably become more open to 'extraction'. Is the scientific basis for a rationale of sustainable management available? Hardly, and it is a worrying situation, though not to me a surprising one. In my various travels in Scandinavia and North America I have come to appreciate the appalling lack of profession-alism in the strategic management of our wildlife resources. While we are still stuck in the Victorian kitsch mode of vermin extermination (whatever a 'vermin' is) and remain deeply concerned over issues of sporting morality they, by and large, have made a reasonable attempt to manage the totality of wildlife resources on a strategic and biological basis. We are alone in Scotland in not having national parks, though I have my doubts over the value of the English model. Personally I do not think that Scotland needs national parks, but what I feel all the countries of the UK need is a professional wildlife service at least the equal in quality to the American state and federal systems. The creation of Scottish Natural Heritage from the old Nature Conservancy Council and Countryside Commission for Scotland was a beginning, but sadly the amalgamation did not include the Forestry Commission and fisheries research institutions. Management of wildlife resources, including Ferox, would then be part of a holistic approach, at least on paper. In the meantime we just have to make the best of it.

This of course is a major strategic and political issue, but we as anglers are entitled to lobby and vote as much as any other group in society, and with angling being the largest participation sport in the country we have potentially a powerful voice. It is essential that at a time when we are under threat from a number of different sources we support one another in the pursuit of the various fish species that make us tick as anglers and human beings, and protect the environment which provides our sport. Anglers were conservationists long before the word came in to vogue. Regardless of the discipline of angling that turns us on and where we fish, we should support our fellow devotees and bury the many differences of approach that currently separate us. These differences are part of the enjoyable diversity of angling. There is no way that carp specialists should impose their value judgements on match angling, or the fly fisherman on the pike angler. We should give one another some leeway and appreciation of what we are about regardless of the branch of angling we participate in. It saddens me however to see the way some aspects of put-and-take fishing have developed in game angling, or the way specimen coarse fish are imported from the continent in order to claim a new British record. This form of value judgement of success lets us all down and plays into the hands of our opponents. The catch and release argument in game fishing has been to me one of the most sterile and negative to curse angling. Cultural values from other societies and environments are applied willy-nilly without due regard to local circumstances. Stan Headley of Orkney summarised this neatly in relation to the management of wild brown trout in the Highlands when he wrote in a 1993 issue of a prominent angling journal: 'A new breed of angling commentator has appeared on the scene who considers it anathema ever to kill a fish.' I share Stan's concerns about this because there is room for a kitchen table cull in many Highland lochs. This is of course true for much of Ireland and parts of England and Wales. To me it is another facet of the way some inhabitants of the southern parts of Britain misunderstand the north both environmentally and culturally. This misunderstanding applies to Ferox and charr also. The source of this misunderstanding is to my mind either simple or wilful ignorance. Some of the former is forgivable, bearing in mind the failings of fisheries biologists I mentioned in the introduction; the latter will require a more robust approach as it is dangerous to the future well-being of Ferox.

Several times in the text I have mentioned the Ferox-85 Group and perhaps many of you are wondering about the nature of the organisation. One of its main objectives was to remove some of the ignorance about Ferox which clouds the prospect for their future management. This is directly linked to another objective of finding out more about the angling approach necessary. In its psychology it has many parallels with carp and pike specimen groups rather than with other branches of game angling.

The group was formed in June 1985 on the banks of Loch Quoich in Inverness-shire during the aftermath of a week-long attempt to catch a British record trout, sponsored by a major whisky firm. The attempt failed, but the week generated amongst the motley collection of experienced loch anglers and freshwater biologists a fierce desire to know more about the basic biology of the fish and the methods needed to catch them. It became very obvious during the week that both areas of knowledge needed major inputs because for at least half the time we were quite simply guessing; myth, tradition and faith were not enough on which to base a record attempt. Therefore the group was constituted to advance both the sporting and scientific knowledge of the fish. Central to this was a desire to have the irrational prejudice exhibited against Ferox, in some quarters, counteracted by facts, on the basis that truth is the enemy of bigotry. In this the experience of pike-specimen groups was borne in mind and the success they have had in turning round public perception of their preferred sporting quarry. In order to promulgate the intrinsic and conservational value of Ferox we have deliberately sought media attention. No false modesty here, for by any yardstick we have been fairly successful. We do not however primarily function as an angling promotional venture. Our success in promulgating our view, especially since the capture of the British record, has meant that as secretary I am faced with frequent applications for membership. Well, I am afraid to say that amongst our other noble aims there is no desire to function as an open democratic unit. Membership is by invitation only. We are in fact an élitist cabal, but we could not care less about social status, race, creed, religion, sex or worldly wealth. (However, if you own a fishing tackle company, a whisky distillery and a chandlers we would be most interested to hear from you!)

A main part of our remit is to assist those engaged in research into Ferox or their environment and we maintain a strong contact with a number of institutions and individuals in this sphere of science. This is not purely altruistic by any means. Our Ferox fishing has directly benefited from it. Only by adding to the 'account' can we withdraw from it. In so doing we have to kill some fish. This is not done wantonly nor without gain to the corpus of science, or indeed to culinary experience. This last dispels another one of the 'Scotch myths' surrounding Ferox. They are in fact excellent food when in good condition and, in my opinion, rival the best salmon or sea-trout. They have firm red flesh from concentration of the carotene contained in charr that have been feeding on crustaceans. We have learned to appreciate Ferox not only for the good days' sport they have given us but for the good meal at the end of it too, pleasures available only for as long as we look after their primary food source.

This brings me conveniently to charr. By and large the basic food source of Ferox in the British Isles is this fish. Ferox do consume other species, but only in the few places in the British Isles that contain vendace, powan, pollan or planktivorous trout do they have access to alternative substantial populations of pelagic fish. In this we have a simpler picture than our Scandinavian cousins who have to take into account in their management programmes not only the prospect of managing these species above, but also land-locked smelt. This is made even more difficult when several of these prey species occur in the same lake and there is a complicated set of interactions not only between predator and prey, but also among the component prey species. To this complexity is occasionally added the vexation of other non-salmonid/salmonoid species such as burbot, ruffe and zander.

We have comparatively a much simpler picture to envisage, but one, it would appear, that becomes more complicated the closer it is examined. The trouble is, especially in Scotland, that we have not looked closely enough. The recent discoveries of diverse forms of charr in Loch Rannoch are a timely reminder of this and I wonder how many other lochs will throw up similar complexities, even the occurrence of new forms of charr or perhaps new records of whitefish. By and large though, we will still be dealing predominantly with charr/brown trout ecosystems which are lightly utilised by Scandinavian or Continental standards. Once again, because of the ecological similarities, we can draw on Nordic experience to postulate basic potential and management options, bolstered by such experience as we have in from own backyard.

The practical and utilitarian attitude taken to the management and utilisation of inland fisheries in Scandinavia would come as a shock to the piscatorial prudery that pervades the British scene. It is possible to go into tackle shops in Nordic towns and purchase a gill-net, otter board and fish snare in addition to normal rod and line gear. This can be done without breaking the law or developing any kind of guilt complex. Free from feudal subjection in a way that the descendants of Viking settlers in this country never were, rural communities in Scandinavia developed wild harvest fisheries for trout charr and whitefish in addition to sports fisheries. They co-exist in a way that would be totally alien to our modern British context.

Professor Per Aass sorts the nets on the shore of a Norwegian lake which supports a substantial harvest of charr.

Some echoes of this pragmatic approach did exist in our own past as at Windermere and Loch Leven. There are of course still commercial inland fisheries in Ireland. These past and present fisheries are anathema to most modern anglers and I know from my own personal experience that any advocacy of future fisheries of this sort is viewed very dimly indeed in some quarters, especially those inculcated with the culture of coarse fishing in the south of England.

Before I understood the northern affinities of the Highlands I also transposed the cultural mores of the south to my own local situation. I had this rudely shaken out of me by the experience of seeing fisheries managed for both commercial and recreational benefit in Norway. Sometimes this works well and sometimes it fails. It is however a double option for rural communities as yet unavailable in similar Highland environments.

Bearing in mind our greed and stupidity in managing our marine fisheries it is easy to understand the apprehension some feel with regard to the development of fisheries for charr in Highland lochs. There is no room for the kind of approach taken in the North Sea or any kind of indiscriminate free-for-all. An approach with a sound ecological ethos linked to strict legal and field protocols could, however, offer substantial benefits to upland communities. Right now we have probably the least used and least pressurised charr populations in the European Union. We have on a European basis a rare commodity in abundance and I think we should harness this wisely rather than live in fear of losing it. Currently the general populace in Britain are largely unaware of this potential. This is not the case with our Continental and Scandinavian partners in the Union, who now have the right to settle and work here. Are we ready for the challenge of managing our charr resource wisely, that may come when our European partners realise a potential we blithely ignore? The problem will not go away simply by ignoring it. We require a direct interactive approach to harnessing our heritage.

This was demonstrated to me through my involvement in conservation work not only at Loch Garry, but also by virtue of my position as convenor of Scottish Native Woods, set up by my colleague Alan Drever. This organisation has a specific remit to bring the native woodlands of Scotland into sustainable management. A matter of extreme urgency in view of the fact that only one per cent of the original woodland remains. The reason for this perilous state of affairs is that in the past native woodlands had been considered of little commercial value compared to foreign timbers or home-grown exotic conifers, and therefore had been neglected or abused. The way forward is to point out an economic potential that would generate enough interest to ensure their rational use and prevent further losses. The first act of conservation was thus to promulgate market outlets for the previously 'worthless scrub' and then to initiate woodland management schemes. It was difficult enough to do this with something that was tangible and obvious to everyone, so what prospects for a little fish with a name that sounds like a lump of burnt wood, that most people have not heard of and even fewer have seen?

Well, surprisingly good prospects if we look at the Scandinavian scene and remember the past successes at home. On the same trip to Tunhovdf-jord that opened my eyes to the beauty of Ferox, I obtained a prospect of the usefulness of charr, similar in size and quality to those I had worked with at home, in providing, both by angling and netting, a significant rural resource. Each winter 12,000 visiting anglers came to fish for charr, generating directly through fishing licences and indirectly through local purchases of goods and services much needed income to the local villagers. Prominent in this scheme of things was the provision of lakeside cabins hidden from site in the surrounding forest of Scots pine and birch. A vibrant local economy was in evidence that shamed the economic marginality of comparable places in the Highlands. All this because of the presence of a little Arctic fish we have in abundance yet generally ignore as an oddity. The Norwegian fishermen I worked with in this outdoor university of life listened with incredulity as I explained in my self-taught Norwegian the relative abundance of charr in the Highlands and the almost total lack of use of them.

I came back to Scotland to face a wall of indifference and not infrequent hostility to my aim of establishing similar fisheries in Scotland. I often incurred the ire of certain of my senior officers in the civil service, especially the ex-boss mentioned earlier. In an era of concern over the commercial harvest of salmon and sea trout, and when even work on brown trout was difficult, it proved impossible to convince them of the social and economic benefits of charr. Combined with my environmental interests it confirmed my status as a dangerous dissident. None of the antipathy I received professionally or the venom and nastiness aimed at me from certain groups of anglers has shaken my belief in the sporting and economic opportunity presented by the common presence of charr in the Highlands.

Part of the problem lies in the fact that the potential cropping rates obtainable in comparatively unproductive upland waters are unknown to most people. Because these waters are much less productive than lowland waters there is a perceived problem in taking any kind of harvest at all. Sometimes I get the impression from anglers that the world is a conspiracy to stop them catching fish. To them lochs contain very few charr and even less Ferox. Populations in their minds seem to be numbered in hundreds of charr and single figures of Ferox. Any attempt to harvest will automatically wipe out the stocks and stop them catching fish. While it is true that scientifically detailed estimates of charr and Ferox populations in Highland lochs are conspicuous by their absence, there are grounds for much greater optimism than this dismal view.

My Scandinavian colleagues in the International Society of Arctic Charr Fanatics have often expressed surprise to me that so little utilisation of the abundant charr of Scotland occurs, especially with regard to the nearby examples of the Nordic countries and indeed Windermere. The overall general similarity of the populations in hydro-electric reservoirs to those in the Scandinavian equivalents leads to the possibility of implementing similar uses. The problem in such lakes is not a shortage of charr, but an over-abundance. Management protocols, including the stocking of Ferox, are aimed at either resolving the problem or at least making the best of it.

Members of the International Society of Arctic Charr Fanatics gather in Scotland (1992). They were surprised at the low level of usage of Scottish charr.

This over-abundance of charr was the subject of a major research and enhancement project carried out by a number of my Norwegian colleagues in ISACF at Lake Takvatn, near Tromsø in Arctic Norway. This lake, about the size of Windermere, had developed a massive population of stunted fish which matured at five to six years old and seldom exceeded twenty centimetres in length. In 1984 a major trapping programme was initiated in an attempt to reduce the population and improve individual growth. In a three-year period in excess of thirty tonnes of charr, comprising of over 600,000 individual fish, were removed from the lake by the traps. In the third year of the project, changes in the growth of the fish were noted with individuals in the same age classes above showing mean lengths of twenty-five centimetres. By 1989 the oldest fish had attained mean lengths of forty centimetres. This improved growth rate was most marked in these older fish, and there was no significant change in the growth of the younger age groups.

Performance difference was even more marked when mean weights were compared. The average weights of similarly aged fish were several times higher at the conclusion of the trial than at the beginning. This improvement in the size of the charr was indeed profound, with a third of the charr over twenty-five centimetres after five years' trapping, with some fish attaining weights of some two kilograms. Prior to the trapping project few fish over a one hundred grams in weight were taken. Anglers are now expressing new interest in the lake. An intriguing side effect of the programme has been a recovery of the trout population. This is viewed with great pleasure by both anglers and scientists because the local form of trout is an especially beautiful, golden-yellow race with fine spot markings. Previously suppressed by the over-numerous charr it has now made a recovery. Stocking of Tunhovd trout, albeit of perhaps too small a size to be effective as a predator, did not produce worthwhile results. However the larger charr, previously absent, are now becoming fish predators in their own right. It remains to be seen if sufficient pressure will be placed on the smaller charr by their larger fellows to prevent a recurrence of stunting. The scientists concerned are now investigating various management protocols to maintain the improved situation.

Lake Tunhovd is another interesting case in point. The total annual catch of charr in the lake amounts to between five and ten metric tonnes, per year with yields at about 2.5 kilogrammes per hectare. In addition, the Ferox of the lake are estimated to consume about another four kilograms per hectare annually. One can see that the charr are capable of sustaining substantial cropping by man and predatory fish, yet there appears to be too much slack that could still be taken up. The lake has sustained this pressure for many decades, and as well as satisfying the needs of anglers and netsmen has provided sufficient sustenance for Ferox to have attained weights well in excess of 30lb. Evidently there is enough in the 'charr larder' for people and Ferox. The same is probable in our own waters, with appropriate management, but it remains to be seen if we have the imagination and the courage. Right now, charr from natural sources and aquaculture units in Scandinavia are being sold in British supermarkets. These fish are no more marketable or valuable than our own. It seems that our negative attitude is costing us money. We are not getting the true value out of our charr populations, either recreationally or economically, and until we do they will not be safe. The track record of human nature is to destroy what we do not value. Ignorance is definitely not bliss for our charr stocks.

Charr are not restricted to exactly the same set of environmental conditions that Ferox are. While Ferox need charr, the reverse is not true. In addition to the classic 'U' profile glacial ribbon lakes they often share with Ferox, charr have an amazing capacity to occupy a wide range of habitats. While tolerant of harsh climatic conditions and extreme environmental poverty, charr are sensitive to a number of environmental impacts. As their very name suggests, they are occupiers of an Arctic environment and the comments made earlier in relation to the maintenance of the integrity of that environment apply even more strongly to charr than to trout. Cool, clear, unpolluted water is essential for their well-being. This includes especially the threat from acid rain to which charr are more sensitive than trout. Lakes and streams which have been acidified can look deceptively clean and healthy, but the clarity can conceal a charr-less lake. Charr can live in quite shallow nutrient-rich and therefore relatively productive waters provided the climate is not too warm. Loch Meallt in Skye, which lies on a comparatively lime-rich substrate, is an example of this. However in this type of water they are at most risk from another of their 'weaknesses', – competition from other fish species. One of the management concerns at Loch Meallt has been the threat of introduction of brown or rainbow trout. Luckily, the local angling club has people well aware of the special nature of the loch and this has not happened. Should trout of either species be introduced here the charr would most likely suffer, as a reserve of open deep water does not exist in this small shallow loch.

In this type of water the main threat does not come from trout or other salmonid species, but from pike. Introduction of pike to small charr lakes has been disastrous in Scandinavian lakes. It is part of the mythology of the pike anglers' sub-culture that pike are some kind of ecological balancing act. This is simply not the case in small, shallow charr and trout lakes. In Swedish Lapland, one form of revenge on a neighbour who has poached on another's Cloudberry heath (a highly prized resource in Lapland) is to stock pike into the offender's charr lake. The charr, a favourite food of the Sami people, is then wiped out. Something similar happened in small Highland trout lochs such as Loch Choin and Loch Kinardochy in northern Perthshire. Pike were totally removed from the latter by the fish poison rotenone as part of an experiment in the rearing of salmon in still waters. In Loch Choin the rotenone was less effectively used in an attempt to remove pike in order to re-establish a trout fishery. For a few years this worked, but gradually from a few survivors the pike returned to dominance and although there is the occasional trout still caught, by and large the loch is not worthwhile from this point of view.

In some Austrian lakes the growth rate of charr was reduced following the introduction of pike. This was thought to be due to the charr learning to avoid the littoral zone and therefore predation pressure from the pike. As a consequence they had to subsist on the poorer food supply of the pelagic zone. Transferring the findings of research on the role of pike in lowland lakes with their potential prey fish of coarse fish to charr and brown trout lakes of the uplands is inadvisable. In the former we are often dealing with a predator/prey relationship that has evolved over millennia, as has indeed that of Ferox and charr in their own special environment. However, pike are not native to many upland situations and may interact very differently than the way they do in their natural range. In the larger lochs there seems to be a habitat segregation, with pike living in the shallower zones and the charr in the deeper, but pike prefer the same ideal shallow water that trout do. We do not have a before and after situation to come to any solid conclusions about what happened when pike were first introduced to Highland lochs.

Apart from any direct competition for food with Ferox we have to consider what effect pike have on the recruitment of juvenile Ferox to the main piscivorous period of their lives. Pike, like Ferox, have a preferred prey size. If we are to believe the viewpoint of pike enthusiasts then pike would spend their time eating younger pike and the population would be dominated by large individuals. These larger pike are quite capable of consuming thirty to thirty-five centimetre trout, just the size for turning into main-phase Ferox. I know from the work of colleagues in Loch Leven that only a small proportion of the many pike stomachs they examined contained other pike. The preferred prey was trout, even with the presence of a substantial population of perch. The presence, or, more correctly, the introduction of pike into Highland Ferox and charr waters worries me. As a keen pike angler myself I used to accept the role of pike as being acceptable in this situation. Now I am less sure. It would appear that adult Ferox and pike may inhabit different zones of the lake. This seems to be the case in Loch Rannoch and in places like Lake Randsfjord in Norway, but we are still left with the niggling doubt that the Ferox would be more plentiful if pike were absent. Without the detailed research necessary to clarify the situation the debate will drag on. The indications that the pike removal programme at Windermere was beneficial to the charr population fuels the anti-pike feeling in me as does the changed situation in the big Scandinavian lakes. We cannot 'blame' the pike for responding to a physical change caused by our engineering actions, but the biological implications remain. If pike were not present in the first place then there would be no increased pressure on the descending Ferox smolts. Pike in their natural habitat are an asset to be cared for, but their occurrence in Ferox and charr waters where they are present only because of human action is a cause for some concern. No further introductions should be made.

Some pike anglers present another indirect threat to the natural ecology of Ferox and charr waters. Whatever the moral arguments are for the use of live baits for predatory fish such as pike, in terms of individual suffering of the bait fish, there is another deep concern on the broader ecological front. This concerns the release of livebaits after a fishing session. As explained in the chapter on the environment, the north and west of Britain has a very different environmental history from the south and east. This expresses itself in a variety of ways, including the natural distribution of fish species. In simplistic terms the warmer and more 'continental' south and east is the realm of carp family and other coarse fish species, while the oceanic and cooler north and west are the domain of the salmonid species. There is of course a natural overlap in some areas, but for centuries man has obscured this natural distribution by deliberate and accidental introductions of fish, including several species not even of native British origin.

Introduction of various coarse fish species in the Loch Lomond catchment area in the last twenty years has taken place through the agency of pike anglers bringing live baits from their home areas in what has become a pike pilgrimage to the loch by a clutch of enthusiasts from south of the border. Loch Lomond has become a famous pike venue through popular articles in the press extolling its virtues among the pantheon of pike waters. It certainly produces hard, fighting fish of the highest quality and one can understand the visitors' enthusiasm for the venues, apart from their scenic beauties. However, few of the visitors seem to appreciate its natural ecology, and now, because of the release of live baits into the loch, it indeed no longer has a natural ecology.

My colleagues Colin Adams of Glasgow University and fellow charr fanatic Dr Peter Maitland have been at the forefront of research into the ecological impact of introductions of non-native fish into the loch. None of the results of their work helps them to sleep any easier at night. There is now developing in Loch Lomond a potential ecological disaster of worrying proportions. The loch famous for its 'bonnie banks' is also famous in biological circles for being one of only two places where the powan *Coregonus lavaretus* occurs in Scotland. It also is renowned for its excellent salmon and sea-trout fisheries, both in the loch itself and its main tributaries. The loch is also the home of some fine Ferox. These various salmon family fish species are now facing a number of threats from introduced species. Prime villain of the peace is the ruffe or pope *Gymnocephalus cernua*, a close relative of the perch; so close in fact that they can hybridise. This ruffe, unlike many of the introduced members of the carp family, is well adapted to the physical conditions found in the glacial lochs of the uplands. Indeed it may sometimes be called colloquially in the Nordic countries the 'Arctic perch'. Its physiological suitability to low temperatures means that it has a capacity to feed actively during winter. This is of grave concern to those like Dr Adams and Dr Maitland engaged in the conservation and study of the rare powan. Ruffe, though basically carnivorous, are very selective in their choice of food and are especially fond of fish eggs. This is bad news for the winter spawning powan. It is known from studies in Russian lakes that ruffe have an important controlling effect on the population size of whitefishes. The powan in Loch Lomond have not evolved with this pressure on them and the long-term effect on the viability of the powan population may be very serious. We may lose a special part of our glacial heritage for a mess of 'pike pottage'.

The ruffe also feed avidly on chironomid larvae (non-biting midges), a seasonally important food item of the powan, and are also predators on fish fry. Ruffe, then, are a multiple liability to the future of powan. Ferox in Loch Lomond used to be called 'powan eaters' locally; how are they faring now that the ruffe population has exploded over the last decade? We know from the studies of the above-mentioned scientists that major dietary changes have occurred in a number of fish predator species, including the pike, and piscivorous birds. Ruffe are now a major component where previously they could not possibly feature. Can we feel as confident that Ferox here have also adapted to the new food source and, even if they have, is their future secure? Basically we are talking about a major change to the whole ecosystem of Loch Lomond simply by the casual and thoughtless release of a few bait fish. This is not the end of the sad story. Pike anglers are still bringing new species with them to the loch. Chub and dace are now present in some of the major inflowing rivers to the loch. Chub are predators of fish, including juvenile salmon and trout, and Dr Adams is very concerned about competition between dace and young salmon. Bearing in mind the lessons of the Scandinavian situation, can we consider any such new pressures on the recruitment of juvenile salmon and trout, including young Ferox, anything but negative?

The worry does not end here of course. As a self-confessed charr fanatic I of course cannot blind myself to the pressures presented to the poor old powan, which in a British context is far rarer than my favourite fish. With a reserve of exotic fish now present in the Highlands it is even easier for pike anglers to further the folly of fish introductions elsewhere. The main threat is now to Loch Awe, home of almost certainly the greatest Ferox in the British mainland. Loch Awe is increasingly becoming a favourite venue for pike anglers and has a track record of producing huge specimen fish, no doubt doing very well on the dangerous incompetence of the aquaculture industry. In 1993, during the pursuit of the record Ferox, I was amazed at the extent of the pike fishing effort on Loch Awe. At Kilchurn, for example, there is sometimes almost a small 'village' of brolly-bivvies providing simple comfort for the urban migration from England and the Scottish Central Belt. Apparently the long-stay visitors fish at an array of pike venues including Loch Awe and Loch Lomond. There is therefore the dangerous prospect of a trip to Loch Lomond providing the opportunity to obtain a supply of ruffe or other non-native fish for the subsequent Loch Awe trip. A doubling of the disaster can then be completed in a day, and another ecosystem is disturbed.

Charr are known to be sensitive to competition from other species, and while so far they appear to have survived the introduction of pike, perch and rainbow trout to Loch Awe we have no guarantee that the same will be the case with any new species. Any collapse or major change in the charr population could have the most profound effect on the Ferox population. Even if a huge population of ruffe develops there is no guarantee that the Ferox will be able to utilise them. The lesson of the Lake Tunhovd Ferox, an excellent charr predator, not being able to harness the abundant resources of whitefish and smelt elsewhere comes to mind easily. There is also the experience of North American biologists, related to me by Dr Adams, who found that, unlike Loch Lomond, local fish predators on and in the Great Lakes had not accessed the abundant ruffe population which developed following their accidental release. So far as is known, ruffe have not been introduced to any charr loch and hopefully this will never be the case. The prospect, bearing in mind the past track record of thoughtlessness, is, however, horrifyingly probable. What is really needed is a law banning the use of all vertebrate animals for bait. The debate over how much pain any individual fish or amphibian feels is not the whole issue, though is of course a sensitive one. As someone who hunts fish for other reasons than the pleasure of it I realise the fact that I will be stressing the central nervous system of my quarry to failure. I accept the moral responsibility for doing so. It does not matter to a fish if it is the teeth of an otter or the claws of an osprey that ends its life. There is no reason to believe that my fishing tackle is any less or more of a trauma as predation by these animals. As a native Caledonian I am part of the Highland ecosystem too; even down to supplying midges with sustenance!

No, what is at risk here is not just the welfare of individual fish, it is the functioning of whole ecosystems and the loss of significant populations of valuable fish. I shudder to think what would happen if ruffe were introduced to Loch Rannoch or any other place where charr were heavily dependent on bottom-living food organisms. Many of the other threats to the future for Ferox and charr mentioned earlier are not under the direct control of the individual angler. This is not the case with the use of live baits. I begrudge no one their pike fishing in their natural habitat. I am a keen pike angler myself and I am glad to see pike so highly valued compared to the days of my youth when they were still regarded, especially in Scotland, as that ill-used term, vermin. That they are certainly not, but please, if you are planning a pike fishing trip to the Highlands, do not bring any live fish with you.

So far in this chapter I have given an account of various threats to the future of Ferox and charr. A number of examples has been given of management problems, possible tactical solutions have been highlighted, and hints have been dropped about strategic opportunities and solutions. It is always easy to criticise and much more difficult to propose and then carry out a working code of action, especially if it requires a significant change in political and cultural outlook or major financial inputs. Without all three, the future of our charr and Ferox populations will remain uncertain. If all three do happen then we can look forward to a much happier future for Ferox, and in a metaphorical rather than a literal sense we could have them 'for ever'. In describing this potentially happier future, we can imagine some future imaginary scribe to an angling publication perhaps writing something like the following:

'May is a glorious month to visit the Highlands, especially if you have been commissioned by the editor of a prominent angling journal to produce a series of articles on Ferox fishing in the British Isles. Later this year I will be visiting the lakes of Cumbria and the great loughs of the 'Emerald Isle', but spring in the Scottish Highland is my favourite time of year, and none more so than this one, knowing that I am being paid to do what I love best – catching Ferox!

As I travelled up the route to Inverness from Perth on my way to fish Loch Garry, I glanced contentedly at the sight of the River Garry, just north of Calvine, running full, with banks resplendent in the bright greens of new birch leaves and striking golds of broom in blossom. Not so long ago it was a barren riverbed surrounded by bleak open moor and bereft of its salmon run. Now, thanks to major land use changes and a fisheries rehabilitation scheme, it flows all year round through one of the largest tracks of mixed boreal forest in the country. One could almost imagine one was in southern Norway, especially now that the farm buildings are made of local timber painted a warm, russet red instead of looking like the damp grey Victorian 'mortuaries' of the past. However, it was not the sylvan beauty, nor even the thought of the autumn salmon catch that stirred the pleasure centre of my brain, but the implications of what all this meant for my favourite fish – the Ferox.

With the River Garry, the main outflow from Loch Garry, being restored to something of its former glory, this meant that the major spawning site for the Ferox of the loch was now once more available, after being lost since World War Two. This was of major importance in improving the recruitment of Ferox to the loch, and by the same token the ingress of salmon once more returned a seasonal harvest of smolts to add to the staple diet of charr. This was increasingly obviating the need for supplementary stocking of Ferox which had given the loch the name of the best 'small water' for Ferox fishing in the country. The

National Wildlife Service who ran the stocking programme, in conjunction with the local community, are now phasing the stocking programme out. The potential food source for young Ferox has also improved, thanks to the loch now being surrounded by a mainly deciduous forest which contributes several tons of leaf-litter each year with all its beneficial implications for the production of aquatic insect larvae.

On arrival at the loch I discussed the various management options for the loch with Jim McLaren, the biologist from the University of The Highlands, who did the basic research for the Wildlife Service. Basically he thought that the recovery of the spawning grounds and the improved feeding in the loch would render future stocking of Ferox unnecessary. It was now a matter of managing the psychological environment of the angler and regulating the exploitation rate of both the Ferox and the charr. Part of this was a control of boat numbers on the loch. Only four boats are rented out each day; thus the sense of openness is not lost. Bank angling was managed in a similar way, but a much greater number of permits were issued. The latter brought in more revenue, not just because of the greater number of people involved, but also from the hire of cabins situated discreetly in the surrounding woodland. Demand for the boats is high and the application for the ballot is usually fully accounted for at least a year in advance. That day was no exception and we had our day on the loch, courtesy of the Wildlife Service research boat as a special 'dispensation'. And what a day it was too! I won't go into the typical angling journalist ego trip, but suffice it to say the loch lived up to its reputation and so did the Ferox taken on light tackle. We had four hard-fighting Ferox between 6- and 14lb (I still like the old measurements). The three smaller ones fell to a black and silver Rapala Sliver, and the largest on a small charr kindly donated by one of the bank anglers. The largest Ferox was a tagged fish from an earlier release several years previously, when it was just over a pound in weight – just the right size for starting its life as a wild Ferox. Its parents were local stock from the main inflow burn, which had provided eggs for the regional hatchery for many years. The hatchery reared fish on a contract basis for local communities and was an important local employer. Now that natural conditions have been improved at Loch Garry there is no more need to use its facilities for providing stock for the loch. Jim made sure that all relevant scientific data was collected not only from this fish destined for dinner, but also from the other three which we released. Only one fish per boat is allowed to be retained each day. The tagged fish was only a couple of pounds below the record for the loch so I felt rather smug.

Next day saw me taking the road to Rannoch, to visit one of the most famous Ferox lochs in the Highlands. The management regime here is very different from Loch Garry. Although dammed for many years the regulation level is only about a metre or so and the natural environment of the loch is much more intact. Surrounded by one of the most beautiful mature forests in Britain, it offers tourist and angler alike unsurpassed holiday opportunities, perhaps only rivalled by the Forestry Commission facilities at Loch Awe. This rivalry also extends to the Ferox fishing, and the rod-caught record has oscillated between the two venues for decades. The best Rannoch fish weighed 37lb, surpassed two years ago by the now famous Loch Awe fish of 43lb. Local Rannoch pride is not in the least assuaged by this fish also being the world record. I am afraid that my efforts to help them came to no avail. I had to content myself with a tiddler of 17lb and a fine meal in one of the local hotels. Just the kind of failure rate I like my editor to pay for!

However, even without a new record to my credit, Rannoch remains a revelation. Management of the loch had to take into account the diversity of not only three sub-groups of charr, but also several strains of trout, including two forms of Ferox and of course the erstwhile populations of the main coarse fish species, pike and perch. Erstwhile is perhaps too strong a word for the perch as there is still the occasional one caught, but the combined management techniques of water level reduction after pike spawning time and the use of selective piscicides has now removed this non-native fish from the management problems of the loch as it has done in many other upland waters throughout Britain and Ireland.

Only the outflow spawning strain of Ferox is now reared in the Rannoch hatchery for stocking in the loch. Generally, little direct management of the other bottom-feeding and pelagic strains of trout is required, and stocking of these races ceased many years ago. The outflow spawning Ferox are the faster and larger growing strain, regularly producing fish over 20lb. Their numbers in the loch have more than doubled since the banning of spring fishing below the outflow barrage and the stocking of fish reared from eggs collected from descending adults in the autumn downstream migration. An improved fish pass allows these easier return to the loch than previously, but the returning fry are still hampered by the obstruction. Rannoch is a loch which is the subject of much scientific interest and is part of a joint study project with Scandinavian and Irish Ferox waters. This includes the role of commercial fisheries for charr and whitefish species in the economy of mountain regions. Rannoch is now also well-known for its smoked charr products, based on a harvest of the pelagic race of charr. While not having the time-honoured traditions of Windermere or indeed the size of charr of this Cumbrian lake, the seasonal charr fishery, in conjunction with the sports fishery, brings great economic benefits to the area. The development of the charr fishery is also interesting from a human sociological point of view. Following the entry of the Scandinavian countries into the European Union, the immigration of Scandinavian settlers to the Highlands brought a more pragmatic attitude to natural resource utilisation. The stifling feudal and Victorian anachronisms which suppressed economic and social development for centuries is a nightmare happily long over. Not that the Ferox ever cared about it.

The commercial harvest of charr is something Rannoch has in common with the third and final venue of my Highland jaunt, Loch Arkaig. The least environmentally modified of the three sites I put rod and line to, it did originally have some man-made problems and still does to some extent. All these problems relate to the now deservedly extinct aquaculture industry. Problem number one affected the local salmon. Selection of faster growing smolts meant that the rejects were often just dumped in the loch 'when the boss wasn't looking'; some of the slower growing young salmon were even given to the local angling club for stocking their waters. A genetic time bomb began to tick, the effects of which are still going on. This was insignificant compared to the folly of fish farmers in some other localities who brought in Siberian and Canadian charr in an attempt to diversify during a glut on the salmon market. The superior development of charr culture in Scandinavia made even this unprofitable and the whole venture collapsed, but not unfortunately before damage to the cages had released thousands of fish into the lochs concerned. In one of these localities a genetically unique race of charr was lost because of cross-breeding. Thankfully no viral and bacterial diseases were imported, because of strict veterinary regulations.

Arkaig has long lost these visual and biological scars and is now run as a natural salmonid fishery, and no stocking is deemed necessary. With fine salmon runs and plenty of sea trout as well as free-rising brownies it is a sport fisher's paradise. The charr, together with the salmon and sea trout smolts, provide a rich forage base for the loch's stock of Ferox. While not producing the giants of Awe or Rannoch, there is a good head of fish between 15- and 20lb. The loch record is just over 22lb. Very different in appearance from the Grampian Ferox, being silvery grey rather than bronze, they fight just as hard. Rather stupidly I chose to use the same light tackle employed at Loch Garry, and while adequate for two fish of 8- and 9lb, which I voluntarily released, it was not up to the task of bringing in a large double-figure fish which escaped me near the boat. The one that deserved to get away, I suppose. One thing we cannot get away from is the fact that the Ferox fishing of the British Isles is among one of the greatest angling experiences in Europe. Yet it is only a relatively short time ago that we had almost forgotten about them. There is a book in all this for someone to write, but for now let us hope we have them for ever.'

Suggested Reading List

Rather than the normal format of producing a standard bibliography, I have suggested a reading list for those wishing to further their knowledge of Ferox trout. This is not an escape mechanism for me in terms of the work. Rather it reflects the lack of published material specific to Ferox. A selection of the main popular and general material is suggested as a starting point and a separate list of pertinent scientific material is included as an introduction to the more academically inclined reader. From here the journey to more knowledge is in your own hands. You will never be satisfied, but I hope you will enjoy the frustration as much as I have done!

GENERAL INTEREST

Ade R. 1989 *The Trout and Salmon Handbook: a guide to the wild fish* London: Christopher Helm.

Berkenhout, J. 1789 *Synopsis of the natural history of Great Britain and Ireland* Vol.I. London: Cadell

Bailey, J. 1991 *Casting for Gold* Crowood Press

Bailey, J. 1993 *Our decision. Salmon & Trout* winter 1993, page 73

Begbie, E. 1994 *Don't load the gun for the antis* Salmon & Trout, May–June 1994 page 30

Campbell, R.N. 1963 *Ferox in Highland lochs Rod and Line.* 2.

Colqhoun, J. 1888 *The Moor and the Loch* Edinburgh: Blackwood

Cramb, A. 1991 *The special lure of monster fishing The Scotsman* 8 Sept 1991 page 18

Darling, F.F. & Boyd, J.M. 1964 *The Highlands and Islands* London: Collins

Day, F. 1887 *British and Irish Salmonidae* London: Williams and Northgate

Frost, W.E. and Brown, M.E. 1967 *The Trout* London: Collins

Greenhalgh M. 1992 *Wild mean and mighty Country Life* August 1993

Greer R.B. 1993 *The monster of Loch Awe Trout and Salmon,* June 1993, page 91.

Greer, R.B. 1993 *Last Chance for Scottish Charr Salmon and Trout* autumn 1993 edition

Greer, R.B. 1994 *Glacial Gift for the Gourmet Scottish Field* Feb 1994, pp 22–23

Greer, R.B. 1995 *Fish take a battering The Scotsman Environment Magazine* 14 Jan 1995, page 14

Gunther, A.C.L.G. 1880 *An introduction to the study of fishes* Edinburgh: Adam and Charles Black

Hardie, J.E. 1940 *Ferox and char in the lochs of Scotland* Edinburgh: Oliver & Boyd

Headley, S. 1993 *To cull or not to cull Trout and Salmon* June 1993, page 95

Houghton, W. 1879 *British freshwater fishes* London: Mackenzie

Larsen J.A. 1980 *The Boreal Ecosystem* New York: Academic Press

Macan, T.T. and Worthington, E.B. 1951 *Life in Lakes and Rivers* London: Collins

Mackenzie, O.H. 1924 *A hundred years in the Highlands* London: Arnold

Maitland, P.S. & Campbell, R.N. 1992 *Freshwater Fishes* London: Harper Collins

Malloch, P.D. 1910 *Life history of the salmon, sea trout and other freshwater fish* London: Adam and Charles Black

Regan, C.T. 1911 *The Freshwater Fishes of The British Isles* London: Methuen

St John, C.W.G. 1878 *Wild Sports and Natural History of the Highlands* London: Murray

Speedy, T. 1885 *Sport in the Highlands and Lowlands of Scotland* Edinburgh: Blackwood

Stoddart, T.T. 1866 *An Angler's Rambles* Edinburgh: Edmonston & Douglas

Sutterby R. and Greenhalgh, M. 1989 *The Wild Trout: the natural history of an endangered fish* London: George Philip

Tudge. C. 1994 *Never mind the Loch Ness Monster The Independent on Sunday* 29 May 1994, page 57

Watson, R. 1993 *The Trout A Fisherman's Natural History* Shrewsbury: Swan Hill Press

Young, P. 1994 *Still Hooked on Scotland* Edinburgh: Mainstream

SELECTED SCIENTIFIC REFERENCES

Adams, C.E. 1991 Shift in pike, *Exos lucius* L, predation pressure following the introduction of ruffe, *Gymnocephalus cernuus* L, to Loch Lomond. J. Fish Biol. 38: 663–667

Adams C.E., & Tippett, R. 1991. Powan, *Coregonus lavaretus* L, ova predation by newly introduced ruffe, *Gymnocephalus cernuus* L, in Loch Lomond, Scotland. Aqua. Fish. Mgmnt. 22: 239–246

Aass, P. 1984. Management and utilization of Arctic charr in Norwegian dhyroelectric reservoirs. pp.277–291. In **L.Johnson and B.L. Burns**(eds). Biology of the Arctic charr. Proc. Int. Symp on Arctic charr, Winnipeg 1981. Univ Manitoba Press, Winnipeg

Baroudy, E. and Elliot, J.M. 1994. Critical thermal limits for juvenile Arctic charr *Salvelinus alpinus*. J. Fish. Biol. 45: 1041–1053

Campbell, R.N. 1979. Ferox trout, *Salmo trutta* L., and charr, *Salvelinus alpinus* L. In Scottish lochs, J. Fish. Biol. 14, 1–29

Ferguson, A. 1985. Lough Melvin: a unique fish community. Royal Dublin Society, Ireland

Frost, W.E. 1951. Some observations on the biology of the charr, *Salvelinus willughbii* Gunther, of Windermere. Verh. Internat Verein. Limnol. 11 105 110

Frost W.E. 1965. Breeding habits of the Windermere charr, *Salvelinus willughbii* Gunther, and their bearing on the speciation of these fish. Proc. Roy. Soc. Loch, B 163: 232–284

Frost W.E. 1977. The food of charr, Salvelinus willughbii, Gunther, in Windermere. J. Fish Biol. 11 531–547

Gardner, A.S., Walker A.F. & Greer R.B. 1988. Morphometric analysis of two ecologically distinct forms of charr, Salvelinus alpinus L, in Loch Rannoch, Scotland. J. Fish Biol. 32: 901–910

Hammar, J. (editor) 1991. Proceedings of the Sixth ISACF workshop on Arctic charr, 1990. Stockholm: Institute of Freshwater Research, Drottningholm, Sweden

Hartley, S.E; McGowan, C; Greer, R.B. & Walker, A.F. 1992b. The genetics of sympatric Arctic charr Salvelinus alpinus L, populations from Loch Rannoch, Scotland. J. Fish Biol. 41: 1021–1031

Johnson, L. 1980. The Arctic charr, *Salvelinus alpinus*. In: Charrs (E.K. Balon ed) pp 15–98. Hauge: Junk.

Maitland, P.S; Greer, R.B, Campbell, R.N & Friend, G.F. 1984. The status and biology of Arctic charr *Salvelinus alpinus*(L.) in Scotland. pp 193–215 *In* **L. Johnson and B.L. Burns**(Eds) Biology of the Arctic charr. Proc Int. Symp on Arctic Charr, Winnipeg 1981. Univ Manitoba Press, Winnipeg

Maitland, P.S. 1990. Threats to Britain's native salmon, trout and charr. British Wildlife, no.1

Menzies, W.J.M. 1936. Sea trout and trout. London: Seeley Service

Nilsson, N.A. 1962. Interaction between trout and charr in Scandinavia. Trans. Amer. Fish. Soc. 92: 276–285

Partington, J.D. & Mills C.A. 1988. An electrophoretic and biometric study of Arctis charr Salkvelinu alpinus L, from ten British lakes. J. Fish. Biol. 33: 791–814

Stephen, A.B. and McAndrew, B.J. 1990. Distribution of genetic variation in brown trout in Scotland. Aquaculture and Fisheries Management, vol.21

Taugbol, T; Skurdal, J, & Nyberg, P.(eds) 1992. Nordisk seminar om forvaltning av storørret (Nordic seminar on the management of large-sized brown trout, in Norwegian). DN-rapport 1992–4. Trondheim: Directorate for Nature management. N–7005

Walker, A.F., Greer, R.B. and Gardner A.S. 1988. Two ecologically distinct forms of Arctic charr *Salvelinus alpinus*(L) in Loch Rannoch, Scotland. Biol. Conserv. 43: 43–61

Index